Autodesk Inventor 2014
Tutorial Book
John Ronald

ISBN-13: 978-1491068731

ISBN-10: 1491068736

Table of Contents

Chapter 1: Getting Started

Chapter 2: Modeling Basics

Chapter 3: Assembly Basics

Chapter 4: Creating Drawings

Autodesk Inventor Tutorial Book

Chapter 7: Assembly Modeling Tools

Creating a Component in an assembly
Creating the Slider Joint
Creating the Rotational Joint
Creating the Rigid Joint

Chapter 8: Dimensions and Annotations

Creating Centerlines and Centermarks
Editing the Hatch Pattern
Applying Dimensions
Adding Hole and Thread callouts
Adding Leader text
Placing Datum Feature
Placing the Feature Control Frame
Placing the Surface Texture Symbols
Modifying the Title Block Information

Introduction

Autodesk Inventor as a topic of learning is vast, and having a wide scope. It is package of many modules delivering a great value to enterprises. It offers a set of tools which are easy-to-use to design, document and simulate 3D models. Using this software, you can speed up the design process and reduce the product development costs.

This tutorial book provides a step-by-step approach for users to learn Autodesk Inventor. It is aimed for those with no previous experience with Inventor. However, users of previous versions of Inventor may also find this book useful for them to learn the new enhancements. The user will be guided from starting an Autodesk Inventor 2014 session to creating parts, assemblies, and drawings. Each chapter has components explained with the help of real world models.

Scope of this Book

This book is written for students and engineers who are interested to learn Autodesk Inventor 2014 for designing mechanical components and assemblies, and then create drawings.

This book provides a step-by-step approach for learning Autodesk Inventor 2014. The topics include Getting Started with Autodesk Inventor 2014, Basic Part Modeling, Creating Assemblies, Creating Drawings, Additional Modeling Tools, and Sheet Metal Modeling, Assembly Tools, Dimensions and Annotations.

Chapter 1 gives an introduction to Autodesk Inventor. The user interface, and terminology are discussed in this chapter.

Chapter 2 takes you through the creation of your first Inventor model. You create simple parts.

Chapter 3 teaches you to create assemblies. It explains the Top-down and Bottom-up approaches for designing an assembly. You create an assembly using the Bottom-up approach.

Chapter 4 teaches you to create drawings of the models created in the earlier chapters. You will also learn to place exploded views, and part list of an assembly.

Chapter 5: In this chapter, you will learn additional modeling tools to create complex models.

Chapter 6 introduces you to Sheet Metal modeling. You will create a sheet metal part using the tools available in the Sheet Metal environment.

Chapter 7 teaches you create Top-down assemblies. It also introduces you create mechanisms by applying joints between the parts.

Chapter 8: teaches you to apply dimensions and annotations to a 2D drawing.

1. Getting Started

This tutorial book brings in the most commonly used features of the Autodesk Inventor.

In this chapter, you will:

- Understand the terminology
- Start a new file
- Understand the User Interface
- Understand different environments in Inventor

In this chapter, you will learn some of the most commonly used features of Autodesk Inventor. Also, you will learn about the user interface.

- In Inventor, you create 3D parts and use them to create 2D drawings and 3D assemblies.

- **Inventor is Feature Based.** Features are shapes that are combined to build a part. You can modified these shapes individually.

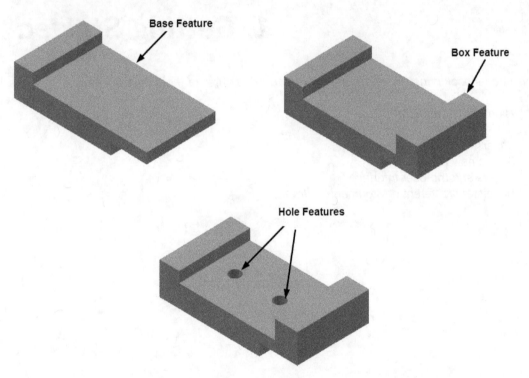

- Most of the features are sketch-based. A sketch is a 2D profile and can be extruded, revolved, or swept along a path to create features.

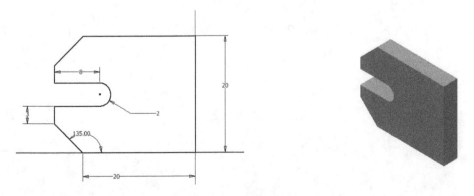

- **Inventor is parametric in nature.** You can specify standard parameters between the elements. Changing these parameters changes the size and shape of the part. For example, see the design of the body of a flange before and after modifying the parameters of its features

Starting Autodesk Inventor

1. Click the **Start** button on the Windows taskbar.
2. Click **All Programs**.
3. Click **Autodesk > Autodesk Inventor 2014 > Autodesk Inventor Professional 2014**.
4. Click the **New** button.
5. From the **Create New File** dialog, click **Templates > Metric**.
6. Click **Standard(mm).ipt**.
7. Click **Create** button

Notice these important features of the Inventor window.

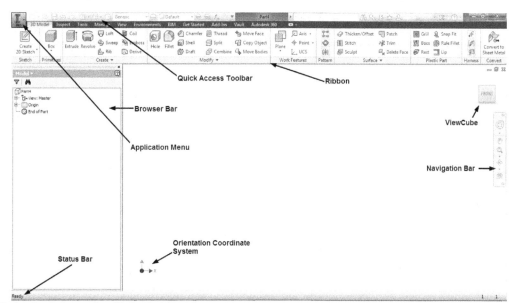

User Interface
Various components of the user interface are discussed next.

Ribbon
Ribbon is located at the top of the window. It consists of various tabs. When you click on a tab, a set of tools appear. These tools are arranged in panels. You can select the required tool from this panel. Various tabs of the ribbon available in Inventor are discussed next.

Get Started ribbon tab
This ribbon tab contains the tools such as **New**, **Open**, **Projects** and so on.

3D Model ribbon tab
This ribbon tab contains the tools to create 3D features.

View ribbon tab
This ribbon tab contains the tools to modify the display of the model, user interface.

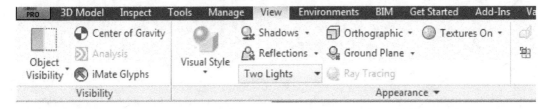

Inspect ribbon tab
This ribbon tab has the tools to measure the objects. It also has analysis tools to analyze the draft, curvature, surface and so on.

Sketch ribbon tab

This ribbon tab the contains all the sketch tools. This ribbon is available in a separate environment called Sketch environment.

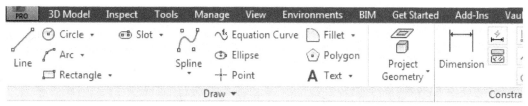

Assemble ribbon tab

This ribbon tab contains the tools to create an assembly. This ribbon is available in an assembly file.

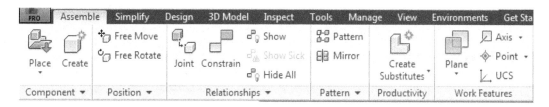

Presentation ribbon tab

This ribbon contains the tools to create the exploded views of an assembly. It also has tools to create presentation and animation of an assembly.

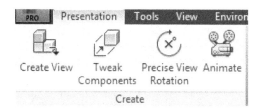

Drawing Environment ribbon tabs

In the Drawing Environment, you can create orthographic views of the 3D model. The ribbon tabs in this environment contain tools to create 2D drawings.

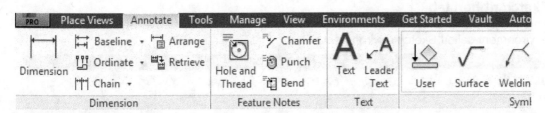

Sheet Metal ribbon tab

The tools in this ribbon are used to create sheet metal components.

Application Menu

This is displayed when you click the icon located at the top right corner of the window. This menu contains the options to open, print, export, manage, save, and close a file. You can also

Quick Access Toolbar

This is available at the top right of the window. It contains the tools such as **New**, **Save**, **Open** and so on.

You can customize this toolbar by clicking the down arrow at the right-side of this toolbar.

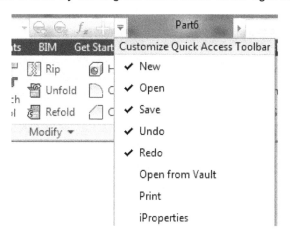

Browser Bar

This is located at the left side of the window. It contains the list of operations carried in an Inventor file.

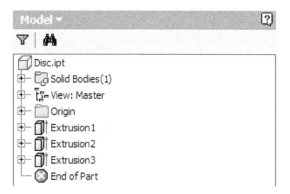

Status bar

This is available below the Browser bar. It displays the prompts and the action taken while using the tools.

Navigation Bar

This is located at the right side of the window. It contains the tools to zoom, rotate, pan or look at a face of the model.

ViewCube

It is located at the top right corner of the graphics window. It is used to set the view orientation of the model.

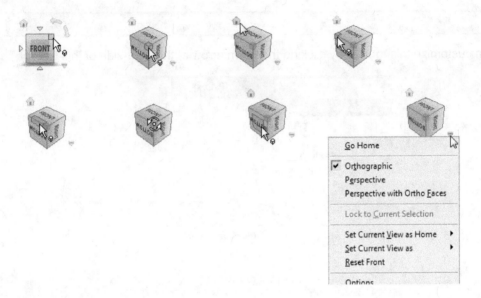

Shortcut Menus and Marking Menus

When you click the right mouse button, a shortcut menu along with a marking menu appears. A shortcut menu contains a list of some important options. The marking menu contains most recently used commands.

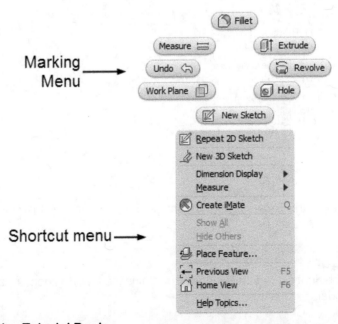

Dialog Boxes

When you execute any command in inventor, the dialog box related to it appears. The dialog box consists of various options. The components of the dialog box are shown in figure.

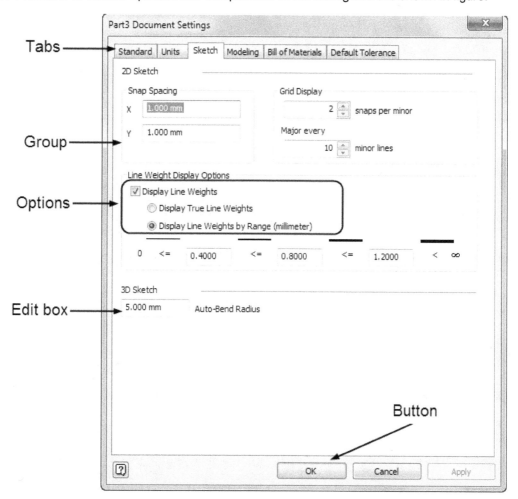

Customizing the Ribbon, Shortcut Keys, and Marking Menus

To customize the ribbon, shortcut keys, or marking menu, click **Tools > Options > Customize** on the ribbon; the **Customize** dialog box appears. Use the tabs present in this dialog box to customize the ribbon or marking menu, or shortcut keys.

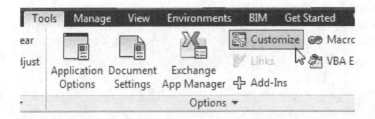

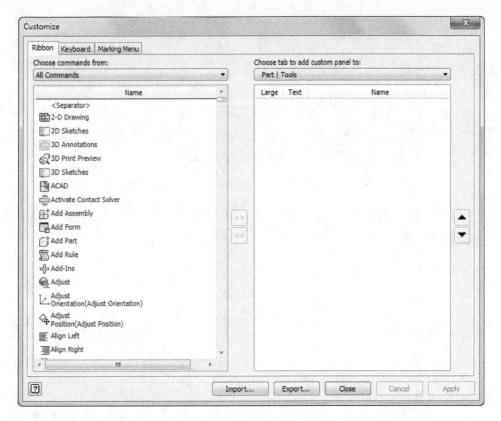

Color Settings

To change the background color of the window, click **Tools > Options > Application Options** on the ribbon; the **Application Options** dialog box appears. Click the **Colors** tab on the dialog box. Set the **Background** to **1 Color** to change the background to plain. Select the required color scheme from the **Color Scheme** group. Click **OK**.

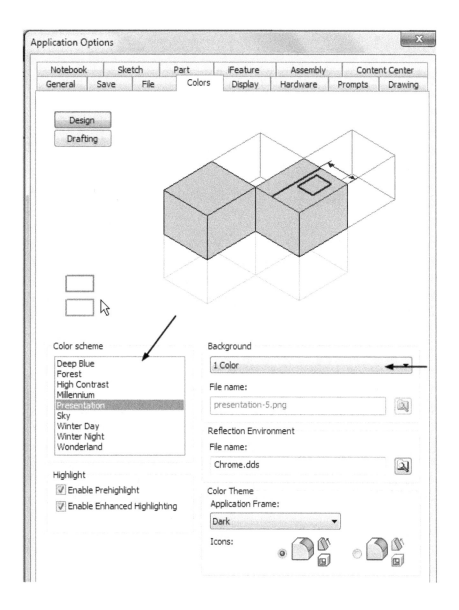

2. Modeling Basics

This chapter takes you through the creation of your first Inventor model. You create simple parts:

In this chapter, you will:

- *Create Sketches*
- *Create a base feature*
- *Add another feature to it*
- *Create revolved features*
- *Create cylindrical features*
- *Create box features*
- *Apply draft*

TUTORIAL 1

This tutorial takes you through the creation of your first Inventor model. You create the Disc of an Old ham coupling:

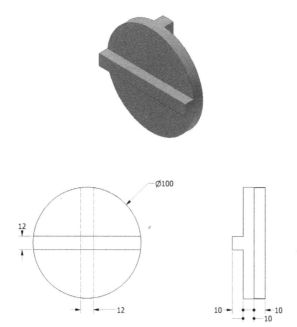

Creating a New Project

1. To create a new project, click the **Projects** button on the **Launch** panel in the **Get Started** ribbon; the **Projects** dialog box appears.

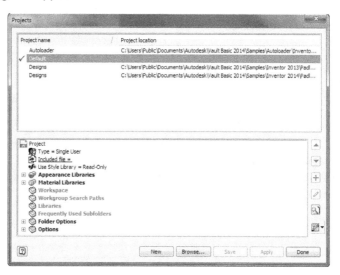

2. Click the **New** button on the **Projects** dialog box; the **Inventor project wizard** dialog box appears.

3. Select **New Single User Project** and click the **Next** button.

4. Enter **Olham Coupling** in the **Name** field

5. Set **Project(Workspace) Folder** to **C:\Users\Username\Documents** and click **Next**.

6. Click **Finish**.

7. Click **Save**; the **Inventor Project Editor** message box appears.

8. Click Yes.

9. Click **Done**.

Creating a New Part File

1. To create a new part, click the **New** button on the **Launch** panel in the **Get Started** ribbon; the **Create New File** dialog box appears.

2. Select **Metric** as the **Template**.

3. Select **Standard(mm).ipt**.

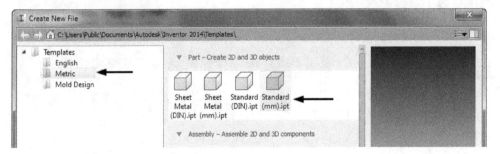

4. Click **Create**; a new model window appears.

Starting a Sketch

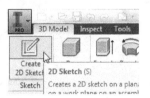

1. To start a new sketch, click the **Create 2D Sketch** button on the **Sketch** panel of the **3D Model** ribbon.

2. Click **XZ Plane** in the **Browser Bar**; the sketch starts.

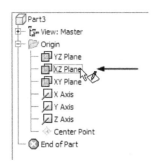

The first feature is an extruded feature from a sketched circular profile. You will begin by sketching the circle.

3. Click **Center Point Circle** on the **Draw** panel of the **Sketch** ribbon.

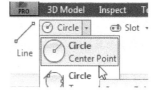

4. Move the cursor to the sketch origin, and then click.

5. Drag the cursor and click to create a circle.

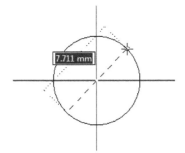

6. Press **ESC** to quit the tool.

Adding Dimensions

In this section, you will specify the size of the sketched circle by adding dimensions. As you add dimensions, the sketch can attain any one of the following states:

Fully Constrained sketch: In a fully constrained sketch, the positions of all the entities are fully described by dimensions or constraints or both. In a fully constrained sketch, all the entities are dark blue color.

Under Constrained sketch: Additional dimensions or constraints or both are needed to completely specify the geometry. In this state, you can drag under constrained sketch entities to modify the sketch. An under constrained sketch entity is in black color.

If you add an more dimensions to a fully constrained sketch, a message box will appear showing that dimension over constraints the sketch. Also, it prompts you to convert the dimension into a driven dimension. Click **Accept** to convert the unwanted dimension into a driven dimension.

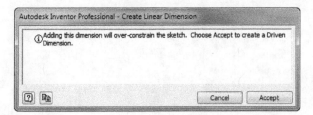

1. Click **Dimension** on the **Constrain** panel of the **Sketch** ribbon.

2. Select the circle and click; the **Edit Dimension** box appears.

3. Enter **100** in the **Edit Dimension** box and click the green check .

4. Press **Esc** to quit the **Dimension** tool.

5. To display the entire circle at full size and to center it in the graphics area, use one of the following methods:

    • Click **Zoom All** on the **Navigate Bar**.
    • Click **View > Navigate > Zoom All**.

    You can also enter the input values while drawing a sketched entity. Enter the values in the edit boxes displayed while sketching.

6. Click **Finish Sketch** on the **Exit** panel.

7. Click the **Home** icon on the ViewCube.

Creating the Base Feature

The first feature in any part is called a base feature. You now create this feature by extruding the sketched circle.

1. Click **Extrude** on the **Create** panel; the **Extrude** dialog box appears.

Autodesk Inventor Tutorial Book

2. Enter 10 in the **Distance** edit box in the **Extents** group.

3. To see how the model would look if you extrude the sketch in the opposite direction, click **Direction 2** button in the **Extents** group.

4. Make sure that **Solid** is selected in **Output** group

5. Click **OK** to create the extrusion.

    Notice the new feature, **Extrude**, in the **Browser Bar**.

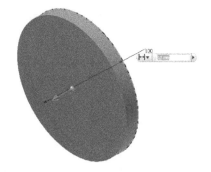

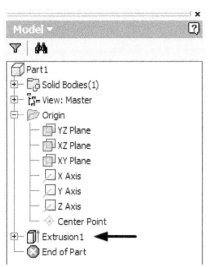

To magnify a model in the graphics area, you can use the zoom tools available on the **Zoom** drop-down in the **Navigate** panel of the **View** ribbon.

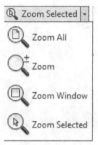

Click **Zoom All** to display the part full size in the current window.

Click **Zoom Window**, then drag the pointer to create a rectangle; the area in the rectangle zooms to fill the window.

Click **Zoom**, then drag the pointer. Dragging up zooms out; dragging down zooms in.

Click a vertex, an edge, or a feature, then click **Zoom Selected**; the selected item zooms to fill the window.

To display the part in different modes, click the options in the **View Style** drop-down on the **Appearance** panel of the **View** ribbon.

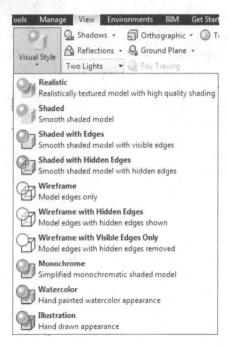

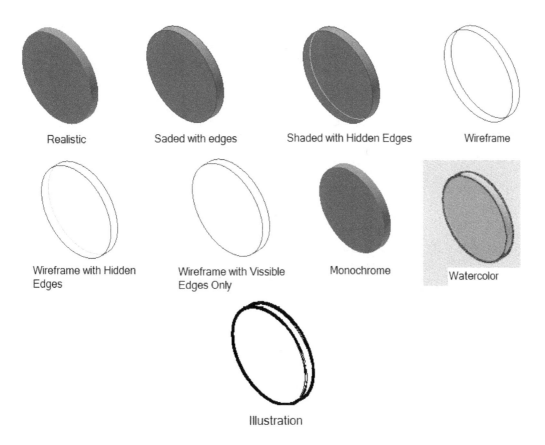

Realistic   Saded with edges   Shaded with Hidden Edges   Wireframe

Wireframe with Hidden   Wireframe with Vissible   Monochrome   Watercolor
Edges   Edges Only

Illustration

The default display mode for parts and assemblies is **Shaded**. You may change the display mode whenever you want.

Adding an Extruded Feature

To create additional features on the part, you need to draw sketches on the model faces or planes, then extrude them.

1.   Click **Wireframe** on the **View Style** drop-down of the **Appearance** panel .

2.   Click **Create 2D Sketch** on the **Sketch** panel of the **3D Model** ribbon.

3.   Click on the front face of the part.

4.   Click **Line** on the **Draw** panel.

5.   Click on the circular edge to specify the first point of the line.

6.   Move the cursor towards right.

7. Click on the other side of the circular edge; a line is drawn.

8. Draw another line below the previous line.

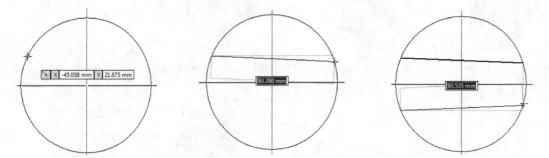

9. Click **Horizontal Constraint** on the **Constrain** panel of the **Sketch** ribbon.

10. Select the two lines to make them horizontal.

11. Click **Equal** in the **Constrain** panel of the **Sketch** ribbon.

12. Select the two horizontal lines to make them equal.

13. Click **Dimension** on the **Constrain** panel.

14. Select the two horizontal lines.

15. Move the cursor toward left and click to locate the dimension; the **Edit Dimension** box appears.

16. Enter **12** in the **Edit Dimension** box and click the green check .

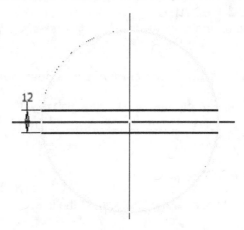

17. Click **Finish Sketch** on the **Exit** panel.

18. Click on the sketch, and then click **Create Extrude** on the **Mini Toolbar**; the **Extrude** dialog box appears.

19. Click in the region bounded by the two horizontal lines.

20. Enter 10 mm in the **Distance1** edit box.

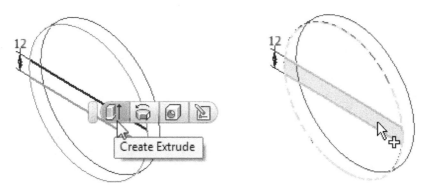

21. Click **OK** to create the extrusion.

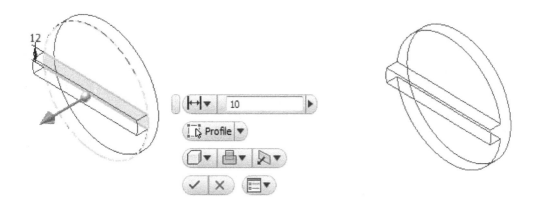

Adding another Extruded Feature

1. Click **Create 2D Sketch** on the **Sketch** panel of the **3D Model** ribbon.

2. Click on the back face of the part.

    You can use the **Free Orbit** button from the **Navigate Bar** to rotate the model.

3. Click **Line** on the **Draw** panel.

4. Draw two lines as shown below.

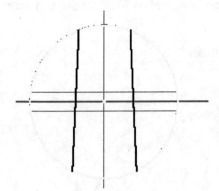

5. Click **Vertical Constraint** on the **Constrain** panel of the **Sketch** ribbon.

6. Select the two lines to make them vertical.

7. Click **Equal** in the **Constrain** panel of the **Sketch** ribbon.

8. Select the two vertical lines to make them equal.

9. Apply a dimension of 12 mm between the vertical lines.

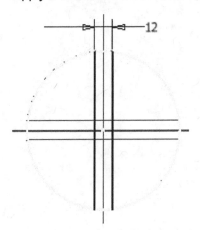

10. Click **Finish Sketch**.

11. Extrude the sketch upto 10 mm distance.

    To move the part view, click **Pan** on **Navigate Bar**, then drag
    the part to move it around in the graphics area.

12. Click **Shaded with Edges** on **View > Appearance > View Style**
    drop-down.

Saving the Part

1. Click **Save** on the **Quick Acces Toolbar**; the **Save As** dialog box appears.

2. Specify **Disc** as **File name**.

3. Browse to **C:\Users\Username\Documents** folder and then create a new folder name Oldham Coupling.

4. Click **Save** to save the file.

5. Click **Application Menu > Close**.

Note:
*.ipt is the file extension for all the files that are created in the Part environment of Autodesk Inventor.

TUTORIAL 2

In this tutorial, you create a flange by performing the following:

- Creating a revolved feature
- Creating a cut features
- Adding fillets

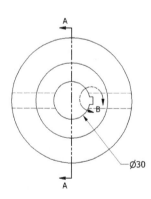

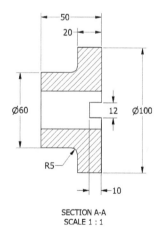

SECTION A-A
SCALE 1 : 1

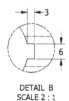

DETAIL B
SCALE 2 : 1

Creating a New Part File

1. To create a new part, click the **New** button on the **Launch** panel in the **Get Started** ribbon; the **Create New File** dialog box appears.

2. Select **Metric** as the **Template**.

3. Select **Standard(mm).ipt**.

4. Click **Create**.

Sketching a Revolve Profile

You create the base feature of the flange by revolving a profile around a centerline.

1. Click **3D Model > Sketch > Create 2D Sketch** on the ribbon.

2. Select the YZ plane.

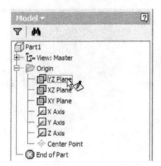

3. Click **Line** on the **Draw** panel.

4. Create a sketch similar to that shown in figure.

5. Click **Centerline** on the **Format** panel of the **Sketch** ribbon.

6. Click **Line** on the **Draw** panel.

7. Create a centerline as shown below.

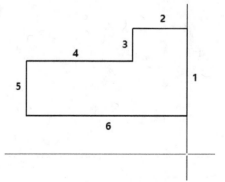

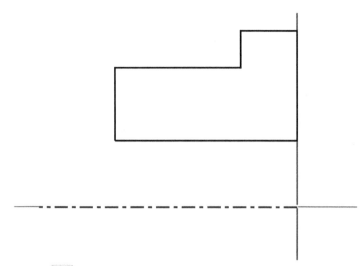

8. Click **Fix** 🔒 on the **Constrain** panel.

9. Select the Line 1.

10. Click **Dimension** on the **Constrain** panel.

11. Select the centerline and Line 6; a dimension appears.

12. Place the dimension and enter **30** in the **Edit Dimension** box.

13. Click the green check ✔.

14. Select the centerline and Line 4; a dimension appears.

15. Set the dimension to 60 mm.

16. Select the centerline and Line 2; a dimension appears.

17. Set the dimension to 100 mm.

18. Create a dimension between Line 1 and Line 3.

19. Set the dimension to 20 mm.

20. Create a dimension of 50 mm between Line and Line 5.

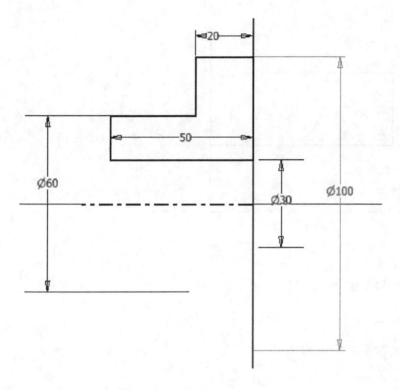

21. Right-click and click **Finish 2D Sketch**.

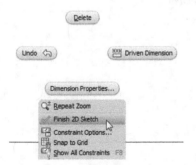

22. Right-click and select **Home view**.

Creating the Revolved Feature

1. Click the **Revolve** button on the **Create** panel, or right-click and click **Revolve** on the Marking menu; the **Revolve** dialog box appears.

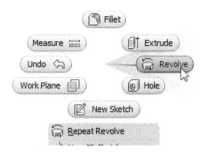

Also the preview of the revolved feature appears.

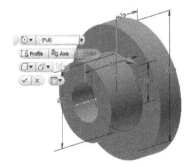

2. Set **Extents** to **Full**.

3. Click **OK** to create the revolved feature.

Creating the Cut feature

1. Click **Primitive drop-down > Box** on the **Primitives** panel

2. Click the back face of the part; the sketch starts.

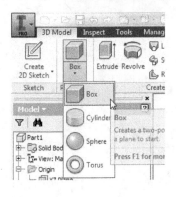

3. Click the origin as the center point.

4. Move the cursor diagonally toward right.

5. Enter 120 in the horizontal edit box.

6. Press Tab key and enter 12 in the vertical edit box.

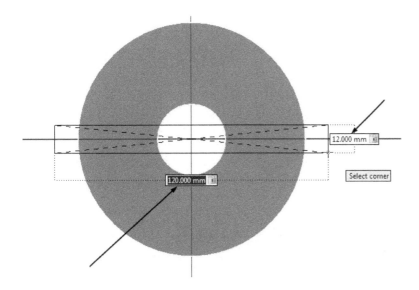

7. Press the Enter key; the **Extrude** dialog box appears.

8. Click the **Cut** button on the **Extrude** dialog box.

9. Enter 10 mm in the **Distance** edit box.

10. Click **OK** to create the cut feature.

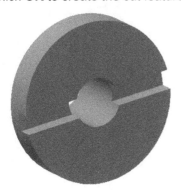

Creating another Cut feature

1. Create a sketch on the front face of the base feature.
    *   Draw three lines as shown in figure.

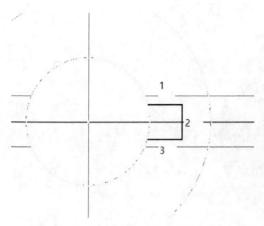

- Apply the **Equal** constraint between the horizontal lines.
- Apply dimension of 6 mm to the vertical line.
- Apply dimension of 3 mm to horizontal line.

2. Finish the sketch.

3. Click **Extrude** on the **Create** panel.

4. Click in the region bounded by the sketch, as shown in figure.

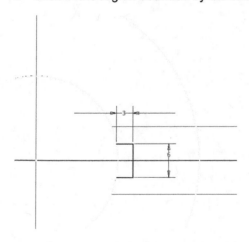

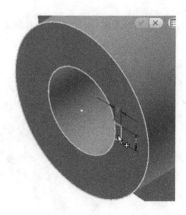

5. Select **All** from the **Extents** drop-down.

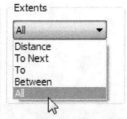

6. Click the **Cut** 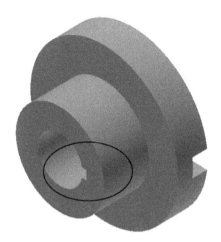 button on the **Extrude** dialog box.

7. Click **OK** to create the cut feature.

Adding Fillet

1. Click **Fillet** on the **Modify** panel, or right-click and select **Fillet** from the Marking menu; the **Fillet** dialog box appears.

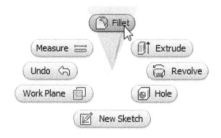

2. Click on the inner circular edge and set **Radius** as 5.

3. Click **OK** to add the fillet.

Saving the Part

1. Click **Save** on the **Quick Acces Toolbar**; the **Save As** dialog box appears.

2. Specify **Flange** as **File name**.

3. Browse to **C:\Users\Username\Documents\Oldham Coupling** folder.

4. Click **Save** to save the file.

5. Click **Application Menu > Close**.

TUTORIAL 3
In this tutorial, you create the Shaft by performing the following:

- Creating a cylindrical feature
- Creating a cut feature

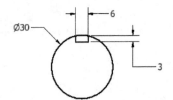

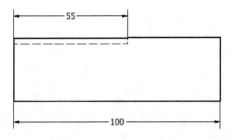

Creating a New Part File

1. To create a new part, click the **New** button on the **Launch** panel in the **Get Started** ribbon; the **Create New File** dialog box appears.

2. Select **Metric** as the **Template**.

3. Select **Standard(mm).ipt**.

4. Click **Create**.

Creating the Cylindrical Feature

1. Click **Primitive drop-down > Cylinder** on the **Primitives** panel

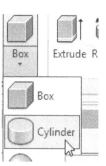

2. Click on the XZ plane to select it; the sketch starts.

3. Click at the origin and move the cursor outward.

4. Enter 30 in the edit box displayed.

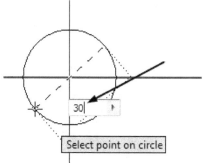

5. Press Enter key; the **Extrude** dialog box appears.

6. Enter **100** in the **Distance** edit box.

7. Click **OK** to create the cylinder.

8. Click the **Home** button on ViewCube.

Creating Cut feature

1. Create a sketch on the front face of the base feature.

2. Finish the sketch.

3. Click **Extrude** on the **Create** panel.

4. Set 55 mm as **Distance**.

5. Click the **Cut** 🖶 button on the **Extrude** dialog box.

6. Click **OK** to create the cut feature.

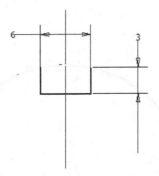

Saving the Part

1. Click **Save** on the **Quick Acces Toolbar**; the **Save As** dialog box appears.

2. Specify **Shaft** as **File name**.

3. Browse to **C:\Users\Username\Documents\Oldham Coupling** folder.

4. Click **Save** to save the file.

5. Click **Application Menu > Close**.

TUTORIAL 4

In this tutorial, you create a Key by performing the following:

- Creating a Extruded feature.
- Applying draft.

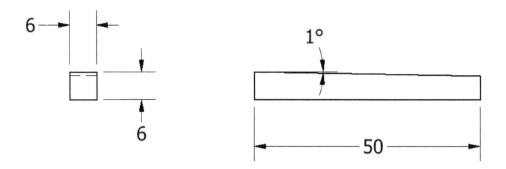

Creating Extruded feature

1. Create a new part file using the **Standard(mm).ipt** template.

2. Click **Box** on the **Primitives** panel.

3. Select the XZ plane.

4. Create the sketch as shown in figure.

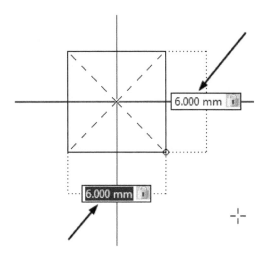

5. Press ENTER.

6. Enter 50 mm in the **Distance** edit box.

7. Click **OK** to create the extrusion.

8. Right-click and select **Home View**.

Applying Draft

1. Click **Draft** on the **Modify** panel; the **Face Draft** dialog box appears.

2. Select the **Fixed Plane** option.

4. Select front face as the fixed face.

5. Select the top face as the face to be draft.

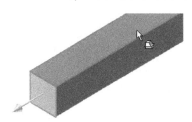

6. Set **Draft Angle** as **1**.

7. Click the **Flip pull direction** button on the **Face Draft** dialog box.

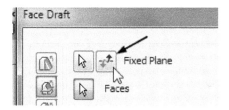

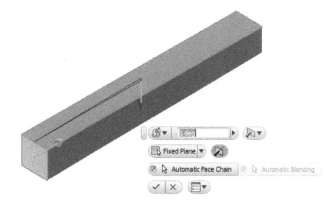

8. Click **OK** to create the draft.

Saving the Part

1. Click **Save** on the **Quick Acces Toolbar**; the **Save As** dialog box appears.

Autodesk Inventor Tutorial Book

2.   Specify **Key** as **File name**.

3.   Browse to **C:\Users\Username\Documents\Oldham Coupling** folder.

4.   Click **Save** to save the file.

5.   Click **Application Menu > Close**.

3. Assembly Basics

In this chapter, you will:

- *Add Components to assembly*
- *Apply constraints between components*
- *Create exploded view of the assembly*
- *Create the animation of the assembly explosion*

TUTORIAL 1

This tutorial takes you through the creation of your first assembly in Inventor. You create the Oldham coupling assembly:

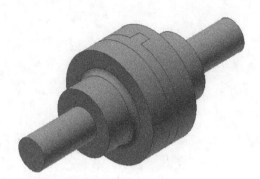

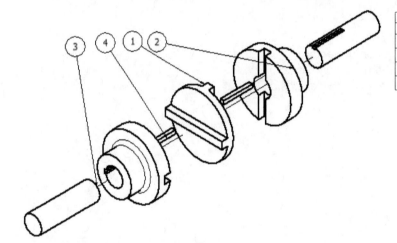

PARTS LIST		
ITEM	PART NUMBER	QTY
1	Disc	1
2	Flange	2
3	Shaft	2
4	Key	2

There are two ways of creating any assembly model.

* Top-Down Approach
* Bottom-Up Approach

Top-Down Approach

The assembly file is created first and components are created in that file.

Bottom-Up Approach

The components are created first and then added to the assembly file. In this tutorial, you create the assembly using this approach.

Creating a New Assemly File

1. To create a new assembly, click the **New** button on the **Launch** panel in the **Get Started** ribbon; the **Create New File** dialog box appears.

2. Select **Metric** as the **Template**.

3. Select **Standard(mm).iam**.

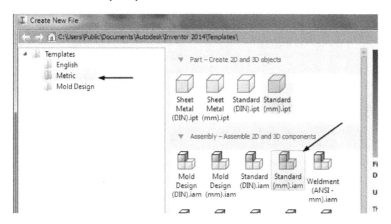

4. Click **Create**; a new assembly window appears.

Inserting the Base Component

1. To insert the base component, click the **Place** button on the **Component** panel of the **Assemble** ribbon.

2. Browse to the location **C:\Users\User-name\Documents\Oldham Coupling** and double-click on **Flange.ipt**.

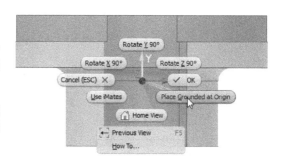

3. Right-click and select **Place Gounded at Origin**; the component is placed at the origin.

4. Right-click and select **OK**.

Adding the second component

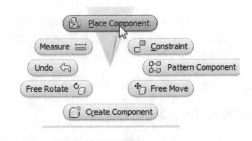

1. To insert the second component, right-click and select **Place Component**; the **Place Component** dialog box appears.

2. Browse to the location **C:\Users\Username\ Documents\Oldham Coupling** and double-click on **Shaft.ipt**.

3. Click in the window to place the component.

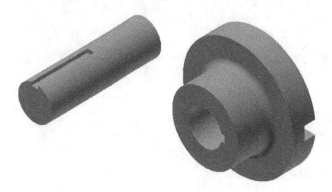

4. Right-click and select **OK**.

Applying Constraints

After adding the components to the assembly environment, you need to apply constraints between them. By applying constraints, you establish relationships between components.

1. To apply constraints, click **Constrain** on the **Relationships** panel of the **Assemble** ribbon; the **Place Constraint** dialog box appears.

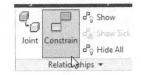

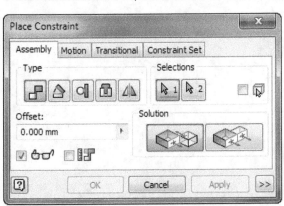

Different assembly constraints are given next.

Mate: Using this constraint, you can make two planar faces coplanar to each other. Note that if you set the **Solution** as **Flush**, the faces will point in the same direction. You can also align the centerlines of the cylindrical faces.

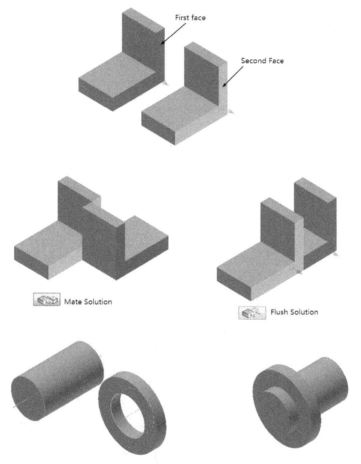

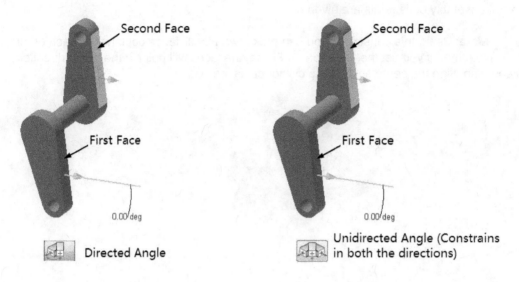

Directed Angle

Unidirected Angle (Constrains in both the directions)

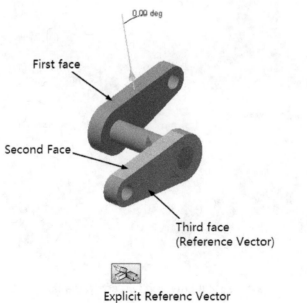

Explicit Referenc Vector

Tangent: This constraint is used to apply a tangent relation between two faces.

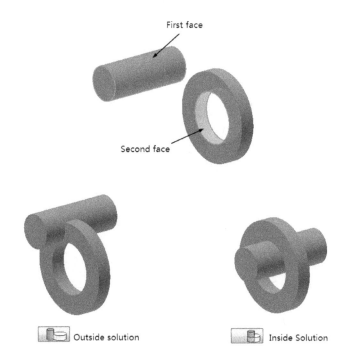

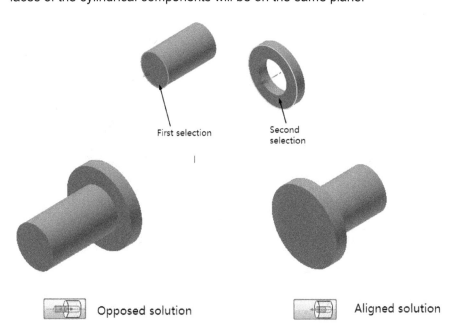

Insert: This constraint is used to make two cylindrical faces coaxial. Also, the planar faces of the cylindrical components will be on the same plane.

Center: This constraint is used to position the two components symmetrically about a plane.

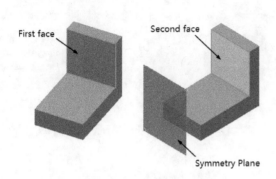
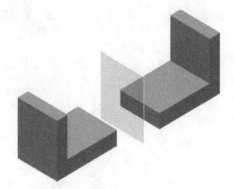

First face

Second face

Symmetry Plane

2.   Select **Mate**  from the **Type** group.

3.   Click on the cylindrical face of the Shaft.

4.   Click on the inner cylindrical face of the Flange.

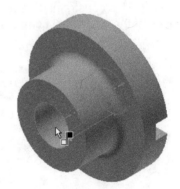

5.   Click the **Apply** button.

6.   Make sure that the **Mate** button is chosen in the **Type** group.

7.   Click on the front face of the shaft..

8.   Rotate the model

9.   Click on the slot face of the flange as shown in figure.

10. Click the **Flush** button on the **Place Constraint** dialog box.

11. Click **Apply**; the front face of the Shaft and the slot face of the Flange are aligned.

12. Make sure that the **Mate** button is chosen in the **Type** group.

13. Expand the **Flange: 1** node in the Browser Bar.

14. Select the XY Plane of the Flange.

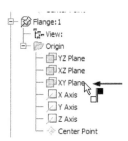

15. Expand the **Shaft: 1** node and select the YZ plane of the Shaft.

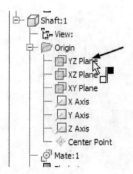

16. Click the **Flush** button on the **Place Constraint** dialog box.

17. Click **OK** to assemble the components.

Adding the Third Component

1. To insert the third component, click the **Place** button on the **Component** panel of the **Assemble** ribbon.

2. Browse to the location **C:\Users\Username\Documents\Oldham Coupling** and double-click on **Key.ipt**.

3. Click in the window to place the key.

4. Right-click and click OK.

5. Right-click on **Flange: 1** in the Browser Bar.

6. Click **Visibility** on the shortcut menu; the Flange will be hidden.

7. Click **Constrain** on the **Relationships** panel of the **Assemble** ribbon

8. Make sure that **Mate** 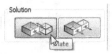 is selected.

9. Select **Mate** from the **Solution** group.

10. Select the bottom face of the Key.

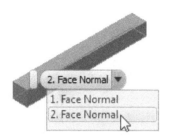

11. Select the bottom face of the slot.

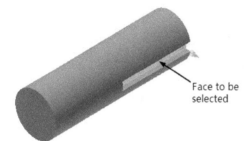

12. Click the **Apply** button; the bottom face of the key is aligned with the bottom face of the slot.

13. Make sure that **Mate** is selected.

14. Select **Flush** from the **Solution** group.

15. Select the front face of the Key and back face of the Shaft

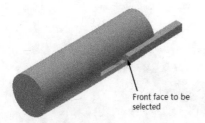
Front face to be
selected

Face to be
selected

16. Click **Apply** on the dialog box; the mate is applied.

Now, you need to check whether the parts are fully constrained or not.

17. Click **View > Visibility > Degrees of Freedom** on the Ribbon.

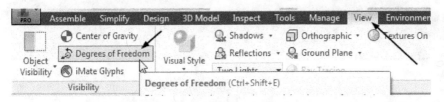

You will notice that an arrow is displayed pointing in the upward direction. This means that the Key is not constrained in the Z-direction.

You need to apply one more constraint to fully-constrain the key.

18. Click **Constrain** on the **Relationships** panel of the **Assemble** ribbon

19. Make sure that **Mate** 🔲 is selected.

20. Select **Flush** from the **Solution** group.

21. Expand the **Origin** node of the **Assembly** in the **Browser Bar** and select **XY Plane**.

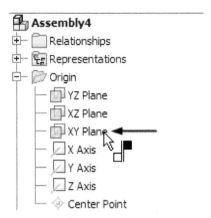

22. Expand the **Key: 1** node in the **Browser Bar** and select **YZ Plane**.

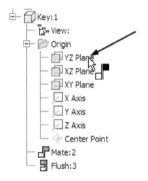

23. Click OK; the mate is applied between the two planes.

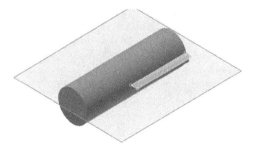

    Now, you need to turn-on the display of the Flange.

24. Right-click on the **Flange** in the **Browser Bar** and select **Visibility**; the **Flange** is displayed.

Checking the Interference

1. Click **Inspect > Interference > Analyze Interference** on the Ribbon; the **Interference Analysis** dialog box appears.

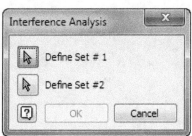

2. Select the Flange and Shaft as **Set #1**.

3. Click the **Define Set #2** button.

4. Select the Key as **Set # 2**.

5. Click **OK**; the message box appears showing that there are no interferences.

Saving the Assembly

1. Click **Save** on the **Quick Acces Toolbar**; the **Save As** dialog box appears.

2. Specify **Flange_subassembly** as **File name**.

3. Browse to **C:\Users\Username\Documents\Oldham Coupling** folder.

4. Click **Save** to save the file.

5. Click **Application Menu > Close**.

Starting the Main assembly

1. Click the **New** button on the **Launch** panel in the **Get Started** ribbon; the **Create New File** dialog box appears.

2. Select **Templates > Metric**.

3. Select **Standard (mm).iam**.

4. Click **OK**; a new assembly window appears.

Adding Disc to the Assembly

1. Click the **Place** button on the **Component** panel of the **Assemble** ribbon.

2. Browse to the location **C:\Users\Username\Documents\Oldham Coupling** and double-click on **Disc.ipt**.

3. Right-click and select **Place Gounded at Origin**; the component is placed at the origin.

4. Right-click and select OK.

Placing the Sub-assembly

1. To insert the sub-assembly, click the **Place** button on the **Component** panel of the **Assemble** ribbon.

2. Browse to the location **C:\Users\Username\Documents\Oldham Coupling** and double-click on **Flange_subassembly.iam**.

3. Click in the window to place the flange sub assembly.

4. Right-click and click OK.

Adding Constraints

1. Click **Constrain** on the **Relationships** panel of the **Assemble** ribbon

2. Click the **Insert** 🔳 button on the **Place Constraint** dialog box.

3. Select **Opposed** from the **Solution** group.

4. Click on the circular edge of the Flange.

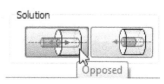

5. Click on the circular edge of the Disc.

 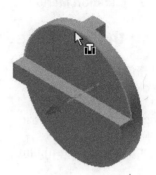

6. Click **OK** on the dialog box.

    Next, you need to move the subassembly away from the Disc
    to apply other constraints.

7. Click **Free Move** on the **Position** panel.

8. Select the flange subassembly and move it.

9. Click the **Constrain** button on the **Relationships** panel.

10. Click **Mate** on the **Place Constraints** dialog box.

11. Select **Mate** from the **Solution** group.

12. Click on the face on the Flange as shown in figure.

13. Click on the face on the Disc as shown in figure.

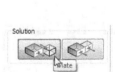

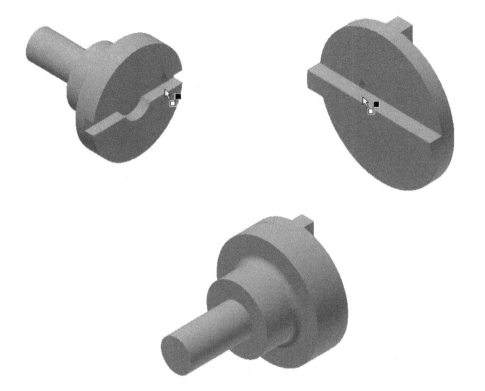

14. Click **OK** on the dialog box.

Placing the second instance of the Sub-assembly

1. Insert another instance of the Flange subassembly.

2. Apply the **Insert** and **Mate** constraints.

Saving the Assembly

1. Click **Save** on the **Quick Acces Toolbar**; the **Save As** dialog box appears.

2. Specify **Oldham_coupling** as **File name**.

3. Browse to **C:\Users\Username\Documents\Oldham Coupling** folder.

4. Click **Save** to save the file.

5. Click **Application Menu > Close**.

TUTORIAL 2
In this tutorial, you create the exploded view of the assembly:

Creating a New Presentation File

1. To create a new presentation, click the **New** button on the
    Launch panel in the **Getting Started** ribbon; the **Create New
    File** dialog box appears.

2. Select **Metric** as the **Template**.

3. Select **Standard(mm).ipm**.

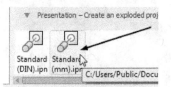

4. Click **Create**; a new presentation window appears.

Creating the Exploded View

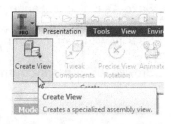

1. To create the exploded view, click the **Create View** button
    on the **Presentation** ribbon; the **Select Assembly** dialog
    box appears.

2. Click **Open existing file** button on the **Select Assembly**
    dialog box.

3. Browse to **C:\Users\Username\Documents\Oldham Coupling** folder.

4. Double-click on **Oldham_Coupling.iam**.

5. Select **Manual** as the **Explosion Method**.

6. Click **OK**.

7. Click the **Tweak Components** button on the **Presentation** ribbon; the **Tweak Component** dialog box appears.

    Now, you need to specify the direction along which the parts will be exploded.

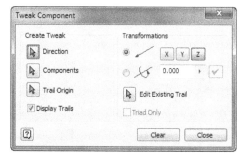

8. Click on the shaft and make sure that the triad is positioned as shown in figure below.

Now, you need to select the component to be exploded.

9. Select **Flange_subassembly: 1** from the **Browser Bar**.

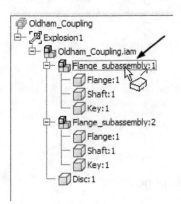

10. Click the **Z** button in the **Transformations** group.

11. Enter **100** in the **Tweak Distance** edit box.

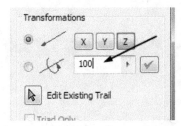

12. Click the green check  to explode the flange subassembly.

13. Click the **Clear** button on the dialog box.

14. Position the triad as shown in figure.

15. Select **Key: 1** from the **Browser Bar**.

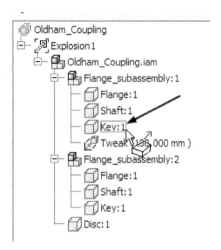

16. Click the **Z** button in the **Transformations** group.

17. Enter -**80** in the **Tweak Distance** edit box.

18. Click the green check ✓ to explode the key.

19. Explode the shaft in Z-direction upto to a distance of **80 mm**.

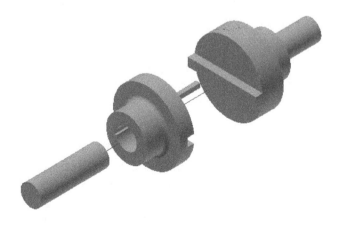

20. Similarly, explode the other flange subassembly and its parts in the opposite direction. The explosion distances are same.

Animating the Explosion

1. To create animation, click the **Animate** button on the **Presentation** ribbon; the **Animation** dialog box appears.

2. Set **Interval** as **10** and **Repetitions** as **1**.

3. Click **Apply**.

4. Click the **Record** button and save the animation file as **Oldham_Explosion.wmv** as the location: **C:\Users\Username\Documents\Oldham Coupling.**

5.   Accept default values and click **OK** on the **WMV Export Properties** dialog box.

6.   Make sure that the **Minimize dialog during recording** option is selected

7.   Click the **Auto Reverse** ⏮ button; the explosion is animated.

8.   Click **Cancel**.

9.   Click **OK** to create the traceline.

10. Click **Save** on the **Quick Acces Toolbar**; the **Save As** dialog box appears.

11. Specify **Oldham_coupling.ipn** as **File name**.

12. Browse to **C:\Users\Username\Documents\Oldham Coupling** folder.

13. Click **Save** to save the file.

14. Click **OK**.

15. Click **Application Menu > Close**.

4. Creating Drawings

In this chapter, you create drawings of the parts and assembly from the previous chapters.

In this chapter, you will:
- Insert standard views of a part model
- Add model and reference annotations
- Insert exploded view of the assembly
- Insert a bill of materials of the assembly
- Apply balloons to the assembly

TUTORIAL 1

In this tutorial, you will create the drawing of Flange.ipt file created in the second chapter.

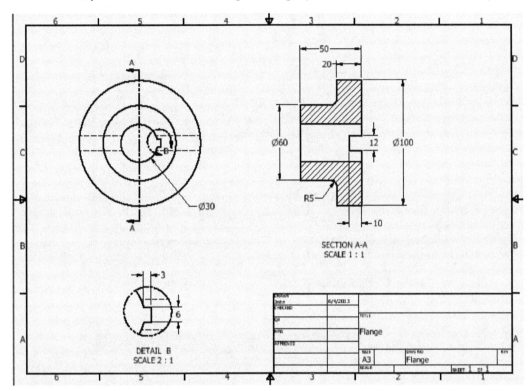

Creating a New Drawing File

1. To create a new drawing, click the **New** button on the **Get Started** ribbon; the **Create New File** dialog box appears.

2. Select the **Metric** tab.

3   Click **ANSI (mm).idw** in the **Drawing** group.

4. Click **Create**; a new drawing window appears.

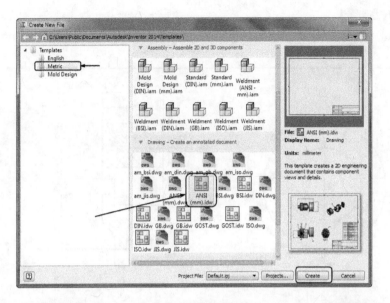

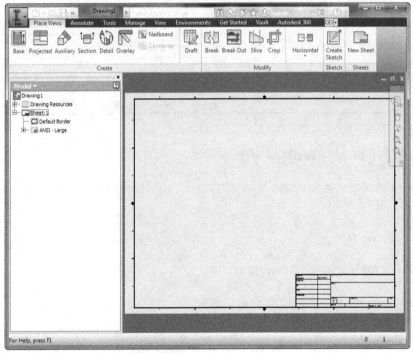

Editing the Drawing Sheet

1. To edit the drawing sheet, right-click on **Sheet:1** in the **Browser Bar** and select **Edit Sheet** from the shortcut menu; the **Edit Sheet** dialog box appears.

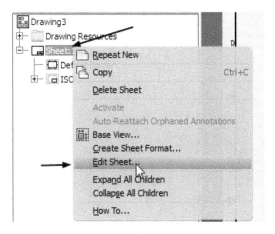

2. Set **Size** to **A3**.

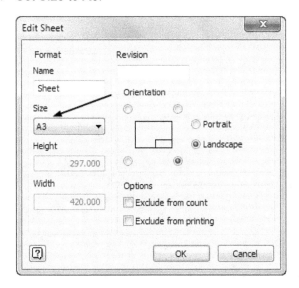

3. Click **OK**.

    The drawing views in this tutorial are created in Third Angle Projection. If this is not set by default, following the steps given below:

*   Click **Manage > Styles and Standards > Style Editor** on the ribbon; the **Style and Standard Editor** dialog box appears.

*   In this dialog box, specify the settings shown in figure.

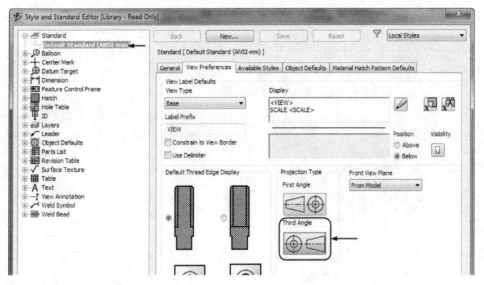

- Click **Done**.

- On the **Autodesk Inventor** message box, click **Yes**.

Generating the Base View

1. To generate the base view, click **Place views > Create > Base** on the ribbon; the **Drawing View** dialog box appears.

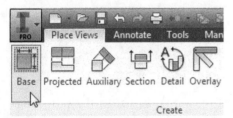

2. Click **Open existing file** on this dialog box; the **Open** dialog box appears.

3. Browse to the location C:/User/Document/Oldham_Coupling folder and double-click on **Flange.ipt**.

4. Select **Bottom** from the **Orientation** group.

5. Set the **Style** to **Hidden Line**.

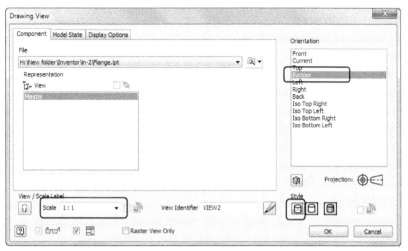

6. Place the view as shown in figure; the **Projected View** tool is activated.

7. Right-click and select **OK**.

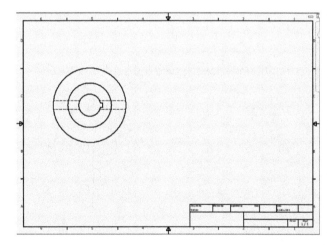

Creating the Section View

1. To create the section view, click **Place Views > Create > Section** on the ribbon.

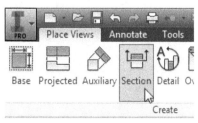

2. Select the base view.

3. Draw a vertical line passing through the center of the view.

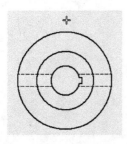 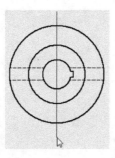

4.   Right-click and click **Continue**; the **Section View** dialog box appears.

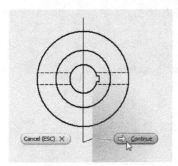

5.   Move the cursor toward right and click to place the section view.

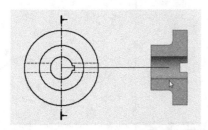 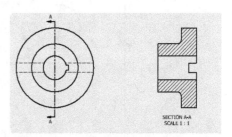

Creating the Detailed View

Now, you need to create the detailed view of the keyway which is displayed in the front view.

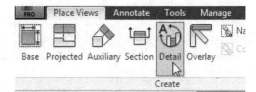

1.   To create the detailed view, click **Place Views > Create > Detail** on the ribbon.

2.   Select the base view; the **Detail View** dialog box appears.

3.   Specify the settings in this dialog, as shown below.

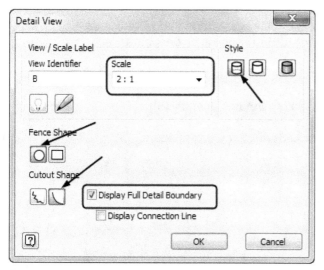

4. Specify the center point and boundary point of the detail view as shown in figure.

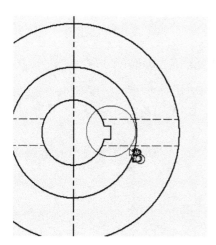

5. Place the detail view below the base view.

DETAIL B
SCALE 2 : 1

Specifying Dimension Settings

1. To specify the dimension settings, click **Manage > Styles and Standards > Style Editor** on the ribbon; the **Style and Standard Editor** dialog box appears.

2. Select **Local Styles** from the drop-down located at the top-right corner of the dialog box.

3. Expand the **Dimension** node and select **Default -mm (ANSI)**.

4. Click the **New** button; the **New Local Style** dialog box appears.

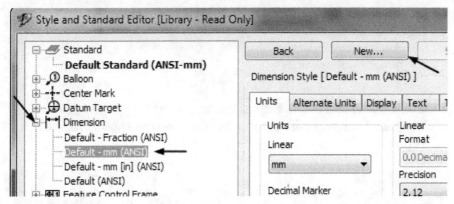

5. Enter **Custom Style** in the **Name** field and click **OK**; the new dimension style is created.

6. Select **Custom Style** from the **Dimension** tree.

7. Click the **Units** tab.

8. Select **0** from the **Precision** drop-down under the **Linear** group.

9. Click the **Text** tab.

10. In the **Text** tab, specify the following settings.

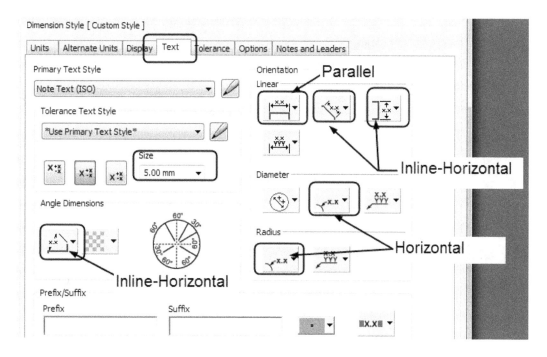

11. Click **Save**.

12. Click **Edit Text Style** under the **Tolerance Text Style** group.

13. Specify **5** as **Text Height** under the **Character Formatting** group.

14. Click **Save**.

15. Click **Back**.

16. Click the **Display** tab and specify the following settings.

17. Click **Save**.

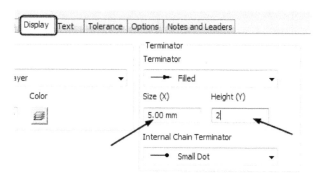

Next, you need to export the dimension settings so that you can use them in other drawings.

18. Right-click on **Custom Style** and select **Export**.

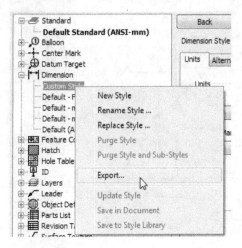

19. Browse to the location C:/User/Document/Oldham_Coupling folder and save as **Custom Style.styxml**.

20. Click **Done** on the **Style and Standard Editor** dialog box.

Retrieving Dimensions

Now, you will retrieve the dimensions that were applied to the model while creating it.

1. To retrieve dimensions, click **Annotate > Dimension > Retrieve** on the ribbon; the **Retrieve Dimension** dialog box appears.

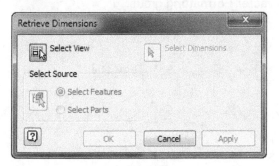

2. Select **Custom Style** from **Annotate > Format > Style** drop-
   down on the ribbon.

3. Select the section view on the drawing sheet.

4. Click the **Select Dimensions** button on the dialog box.

   Now, you need to select the dimensions to be retrieved.

5. Drag a window on the section view to select all the dimensions.

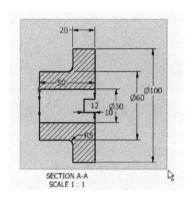

6. Click **Select Features** under the **Select Source** group.

7. Click **OK** to retrieve feature dimensions.

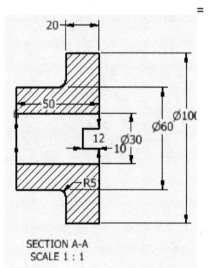

8. Delete the unwanted dimension and arrange the required dimensions as shown in figure.

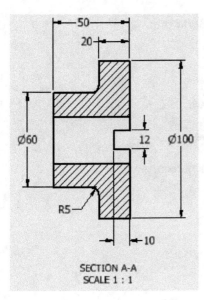

Tip:
• Select the dimensions and press the Delete key to delete the dimensions.
• Click on the required dimension and drag the cursor to arrange the dimensions.

Adding additional dimensions

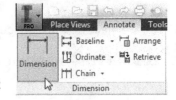

1. To add dimensions, click **Annotate > Dimension > Dimension** on the ribbon.

2. Select **Custom Style** from **Annotate > Format > Select Style** drop-down on the ribbon.

3. Select the center hole on the base view.

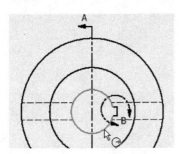

4. Right-click and select **Dimension Type > Diameter**.

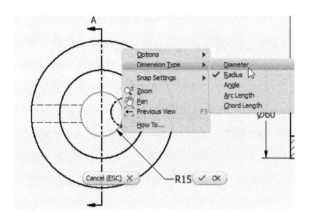

5.   Place the dimension, as shown in figure; the **Edit Dimension** dialog box appears.

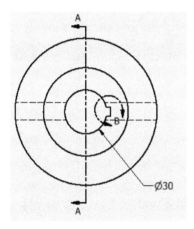

6.   Click **OK**.

7.   Create the dimensions on the detail view as shown in figure.

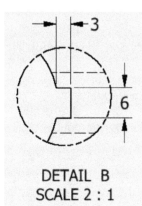

Saving the Drawing

1. Click **Save** on the **Quick Acces Toolbar**; the **Save As** dialog box appears.

2. Specify **Flange** as **Name**.

3. Browse to **C:\Users\Username\Documents\Oldham Coupling** folder.

4. Click **Save** to save the file.

5. Click **Application Menu > Close**.

TUTORIAL 2
In this tutorial, you will create the drawing of Disc.ipt file created in the second chapter.

Creating a New Drawing File

1. To create a new drawing, click the **New** button on the **Get Started** ribbon; the **Create New File** dialog box appears.

2. Select the **Metric** tab.

3   Click **ANSI (mm).idw** in the **Drawing** group.

4. Click **Create**; a new drawing window appears.

5. Right-click on **Sheet:1** in the **Browser Bar** and select **Edit Sheet** from the shortcut menu; the **Edit Sheet** dialog box appears.

6. Set **Size** to **A3**.

7. Click **OK**.

Generating the Drawing Views

1. To generate views, click **Place views > Create > Base** on the ribbon; the **Drawing View** dialog box appears.

2. Click **Open existing file** on this dialog box; the **Open** dialog box appears.

3. Browse to the location C:/User/Document/Oldham_Coupling folder and double-click on **Disc.ipt**.

4. Select **Bottom** from the **Orientation** group.

5. Set **Scale** to **1:1**.

6. Place the view at center-left of the drawing sheet; the **Projected View** tool is activated.

7. Move the cursor toward right and click to place the projected view.

6. Right-click and select **Create**.

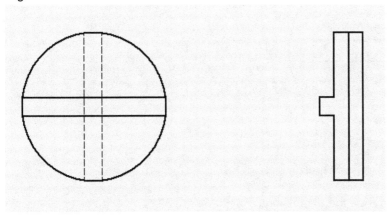

Generating Dimensions

To generate dimensions, first you need to import the dimension settings that you have created in Tutorial 1.

1. To import the dimension settings, click **Manage > Styles and Standards > Style Editor** on the ribbon; the **Style and Standard Editor** dialog box appears.

2. In the **Style and Standard Editor** dialog box, click the **Import** button located at the bottom left.

3. Browse to the location C:/User/Document/Oldham_Coupling folder and double-click on **Custom Style.styxml**; **Custom Style** is listed in the dialog box.

4. Click **Done**.

5. Click **Annotate > Dimension > Retrieve** on the ribbon.

6. Select **Custom Style** from **Annotate > Format > Style** drop-down on the ribbon.

7. Generate the dimensions, as shown in figure.

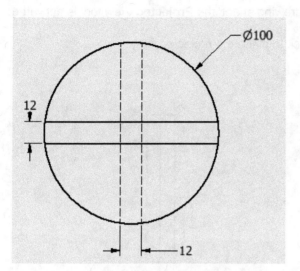

Now, you need to arrange the dimensions.

8. Click **Annotate > Dimension > Arrange** on the ribbon.

9. Select the dimensions of the base view and press ENTER key; the dimensions are arranged.

    Now, you create horizontal chain dimensions on the right-side view.

10. Click **Annotate > Dimension > Chain** on the ribbon.

11. Select the vertical edges on the right-side view in the sequence, as shown in figure.

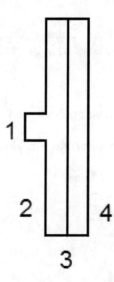

12. Right-click and select **Continue**.

13. Place the dimensions below the view.

14. Right-click and select **Create**. Arrange the dimensions as shown below.

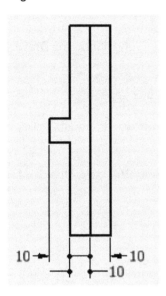

Saving the Drawing

1. Click **Save** on the **Quick Acces Toolbar**; the **Save As** dialog box appears.

2. Specify **Disc** as **Name**.

3. Browse to **C:\Users\Username\Documents\Oldham Coupling** folder.

4. Click **Save** to save the file.

5. Click **Application Menu > Close**.

TUTORIAL 3
In this tutorial, you will create drawing of Oldham coupling assembly created in the previous chapter.

Creating a New Drawing File
1. To create a new drawing, click the **New** button on the **Get Started** ribbon; the **Create New File** dialog box appears.

2.   Select the **Metric** tab.

3   Click **ANSI (mm).idw** in the **Drawing** group.

4.   Click **Create**; a new drawing window appears.

Generating Base View

1.   To generate the base view, click **Place views > Create > Base** on the ribbon; the **Drawing View** dialog box appears.

2.   Click **Open existing file** on this dialog box; the **Open** dialog box appears.

3.   Browse to the location C:/User/Document/Oldham_Coupling folder and double-click on **Oldham_Coupling.iam**.

4.   Click the **Change View Orientation** button under the **Orientation** group; the **Custom View** window appears.

5.   Click the **Home View** button on the **Custom View** ribbon.

6.   Click the **Finish Custom View** button on the ribbon.

7.   Set **Scale** to **1:1**.

8.   Click the **Display Options** tab.

9.   In the **Display Options** tab, select **Tangent Edges**.

10. Place the view at adjacent to the title block; the **Projected View** tool is activated.

11. Right-click and select **OK**.

Generating the Exploded View

1.   To generate the base view, click **Place views > Create > Base** on the ribbon; the **Drawing View** dialog box appears.

2.   Click **Open existing file** on this dialog box; the **Open** dialog box appears.

3.   Browse to the location C:/User/Document/Oldham_Coupling folder and double-click on **Oldham_Coupling.ipn**.

4.   Click the **Change View Orientation** button under the **Orientation** group; the **Custom View** window appears.

5.   Click the **Home View** button on the **Custom View** ribbon.

6. Click the **Finish Custom View** button on the ribbon.

7. Set **Scale** to **1:1**.

8. Click in the left side of the drawing sheet.

9. Right-click and select **OK**.

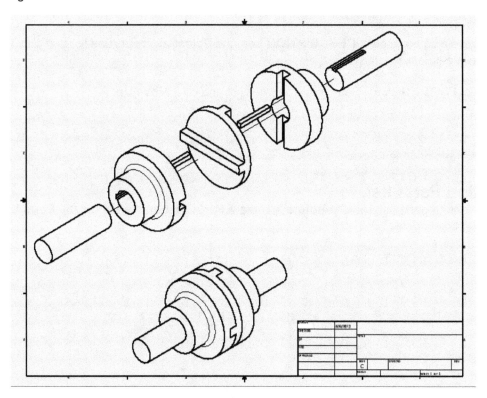

Configuring the Parts list settings

1. Click **Manage > Styles and Standards > Style Editor** on the ribbon; the **Style and Standard Editor** dialog box appears.

2. Expand the **Dimension** node and select **Parts List (ANSI)**.

3. Click the **Column Chooser** button under the **Default Column Settings** group; the **Parts List Column Chooser** dialog box appears.

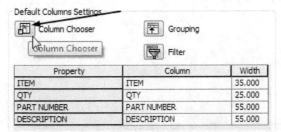

4. In this dialog box, select **DESCRIPTION** from the **Selected Properties** list and click the **Remove** button.

5. Select **PART NUMBER** Selected Properties list and click **Move Up**.

6. Click **OK**.

7. Click **Save** and then **Done**.

Creating Parts list.

1. To create a parts list, click **Annotate > Table > Parts List** on the ribbon; the **Parts List** dialog box appears.

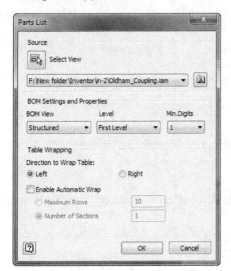

2. Select the exploded view.

3. Select **Parts Only** from the **BOM View** drop-down under the **BOM Settings and Properties** group.

4. Click **OK** twice.

5. Place the part list at the right.

PARTS LIST		
ITEM	PART NUMBER	QTY
1	Disc	1
2	Flange	2
3	Shaft	2
4	Key	2

Creating Balloons

1. To create balloons, click **Annotate > Table > Balloon > Auto Balloon** on the ribbon; the **Auto-Balloon** dialog box appears.

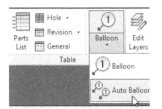

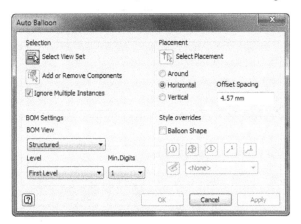

2. Select the exploded view.

3. Select all the parts in the exploded view.

4. Select **Horizontal** in the **Placement** group.

5. Click the **Select Placement** button in the **Placement** group.

6. Click above the exploded view.

7. Click **OK**; the balloons are placed.

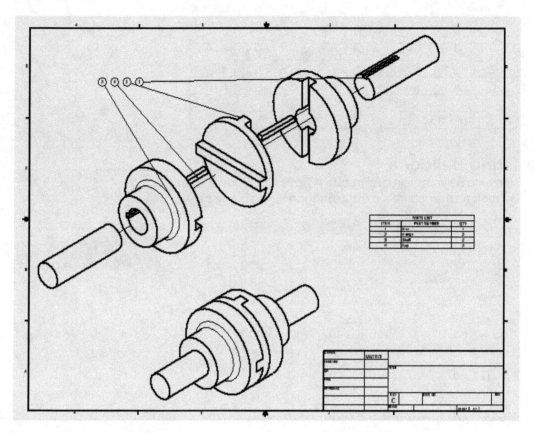

Saving the Drawing

1. Click **Save** on the **Quick Acces Toolbar**; the **Save As** dialog box appears.

2. Specify **Oldham_Coupling** as **Name**.

3. Browse to **C:\Users\Username\Documents\Oldham Coupling** folder.

4. Click **Save** to save the file.

5. Click **OK**.

6. Click **Application Menu > Close**.

5. Additional Modeling Tools

In this chapter, you create models using additional modeling tools. You will learn to:

- Create Slots
- Create Circular Patterns
- Create Holes
- Create Chamfers
- Create Shells
- Create Rib Features
- Create Coils
- Create a Loft Feature
- Create an Emboss Feature
- Create a Thread
- Create a Sweep Feature
- Create a Patched Surface
- Stitch Surfaces
- Create a Thicken/Offset feature
- Create a Grill feature
- Create a Rule Fillet
- Create a Replace Faces
- Create a Face Fillet
- Create a Variable Fillet
- Create a Boss Feature
- Create a Lip Feature

TUTORIAL 1

In this tutorial, you create the model by performing the following:

- Creating a revolved feature
- Creating a cut features
- Adding fillets

Creating the First Feature

1. Open a new Inventor part file using the **Standard (mm).ipt** template.

2. Create a sketch on the XY Plane.
    - Click the **Create 2D sketch** button and select the XY Plane.
    - Click the **Circle Center Point** button and draw a circle.
    - Click the **Line** button and draw a horizontal line on the top portion of the circle.
    - Click the **Trim** button on the **Modify** panel and trim the unwanted portions on the sketch, as shown below.

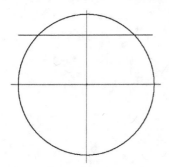 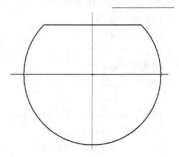

- Apply dimensions to the sketch (Radius=16, vertical length=28).

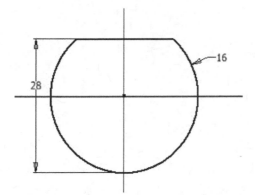

- Click **Slot > Slot Center Point Arc** on the **Draw** panel.

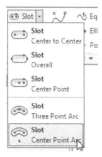

- Select the origin as the center point.
- Select the start point of the slot arc.
- Select the end point of the slot arc.

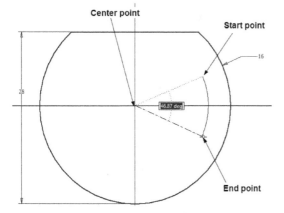

- Move the cursor outward from the arc and click.

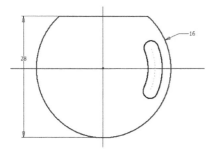

- Click the **Dimension** button on the **Constrain** panel.
- Select the start point of the slot arc.
- Select the center point of the slot arc.
- Select the end point of the slot arc.

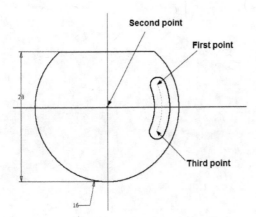

- Place the angular dimension of the slot; the **Edit Dimension** box appears.
- Enter **30** in the **Edit Dimension** box and click the green check.

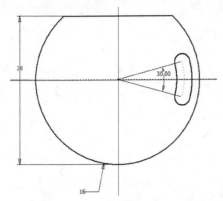

- Click the **Construction** button on the **Format** panel.
- Click the **Line** button on the **Draw** panel.
- Draw a horizontal line passing through the origin.

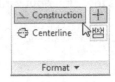

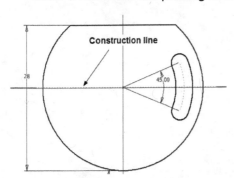

- Click the **Symmetric** button on the **Constrain** panel.
- Select the end caps of the slot.
- Select the construction line; the slot is made symmetric about the construction line.

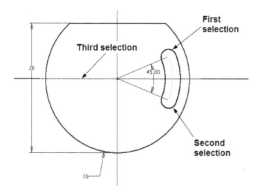

- Apply other dimensions to the slot.

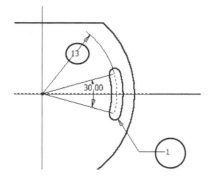

- Click the **Circular Pattern** button on the **Pattern** panel; the **Circular Pattern** dialog box appears.

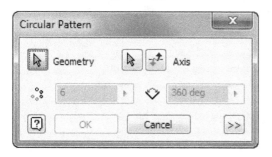

- Select all the elements of the slot.
- Click the cursor button located on the right-side on the dialog box.
- Select the origin point of the sketch.
- Enter **4** in the **Count** box and **180** in the **Angle** edit box.
- Click the **Flip** button.

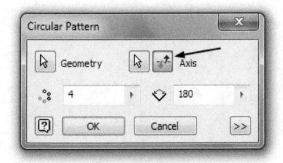

The preview of the circular pattern appears.
- Click **OK** to create the circular pattern.

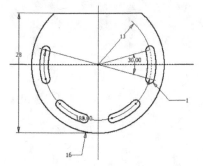

- Click the **Finish Sketch** button.

3. Extrude the sketch upto 6 mm distance.

Adding the Second feature
1. Create a sketch on the back face of the model.

2. Extrude the sketch upto 2 mm distance.

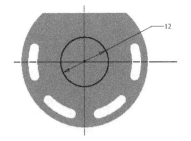

Creating a Counterbore Hole

In this section, you will create a counterbore hole concentric to the cylindrical face.

1. Click the **Hole** button on the **Modify** panel; the **Hole** dialog box appears.

2. Set the parameters in the **Hole** dialog box, as shown in figure.

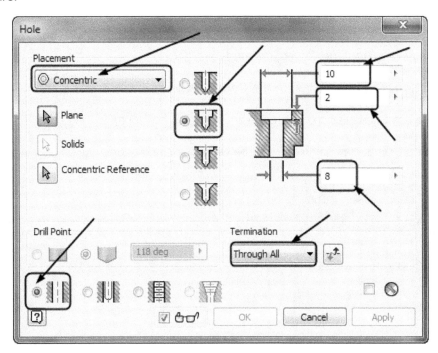

3. Click on the front face of the model; the preview of the hole appears.

    Now, you need to specify the concentric reference.

4. Select the cylindrical face of the model; the hole is made concentric to the model.

5.   Click **OK**; the counterbore hole is created.

Creating a Threaded hole
In this section, you will create a hole using sketch point.

1.   Click the **Create 2D sketch** button and front face of the model.

2.   Click the **Point** button on the **Draw** panel.

3.   Place the point on the front face of the model.

4.   Click the **Horizontal**  button on the **Constrain** panel.

5.   Select the point and sketch origin; the point becomes horizontal to the origin.

6.   Create a horizontal dimension of 9 mm between point and origin.

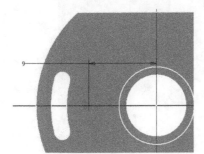

7.   Click **Finish Sketch**.

8.   Click the **Hole** button on the **Modify** panel; the **Hole** dialog box appears.

9.   Set the parameters in the **Hole** dialog box.
   •   Select **From Sketch** from the **Placement** drop-down list.
   •   Select the **Counterbore** option.

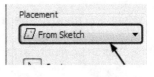

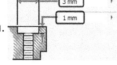

- Set the **Counterbore Diameter** to 3 mm.
- Set the **Counterbore Depth** to 1 mm.
- Select the **Tapped Hole** option.

- Set the **Thread Type** to **ANSI Metric M Profile**.

- Set the **Size** to **2**.

- Set the **Designation** to **M2x0.4**.

- Select the **Full Depth** option.
- Set the **Direction** to **Right Hand**.

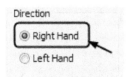

10. Click **OK** to create the hole.

Creating a Circular Pattern

1. Click the **Circular Pattern** button on the **Pattern** panel; the **Circular Pattern** dialog box appears.

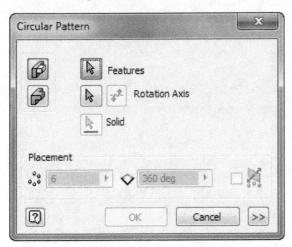

2. Select the threaded hole created in the previous section.

3. Click the **Rotation Axis** button on the dialog box.

4. Select any of the cylindrical faces of the model.

5. Enter **6** in the **Occurence** box and **360** in the **Angle** box.

6. Click **OK** to create the circular pattern.

Creating Chamfers

1. Click the **Chamfer** button on the **Modify** panel; the **Chamfer** dialog box appears.

2. Click the **Distance and Angle** button on the dialog box.

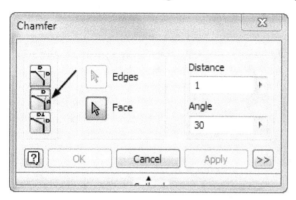

3. Select the cylindrical face of the counterbore hole at the center.

4. Select the circular edge of the counterbore hole.

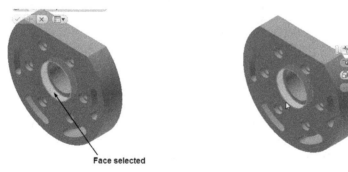

Face selected

5. Enter 1 in the **Distance** box and 30 in the **Angle** box.

6. Click **OK** to create the chamfer.

Saving the part

1. Click **Save** on the **Quick Acces Toolbar**; the **Save As** dialog box appears.

2. Specify **Adaptor Plate** as **File name**.

Autodesk Inventor Tutorial Book

3. Browse to **C:\Users\Username\Documents\Part Modeling** folder.

4. Click **Save** to save the file.

5. Click **Application Menu > Close**.

TUTORIAL 2
In this tutorial, you will create the model shown in figure.

Creating the first feature
1. Open a new Inventor part file using the **Standard (mm).ipt** template.

2. Click **3D Model > Sketch > Create 2D Sketch** on the ribbon.

3. Select the YZ plane.

4. Draw an L-shaped sketch using the **Line** tool and dimension it.

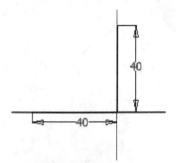

5. Click the **Offset** button on the **Modify** panel.

6. Select the sketch and specify the offset position.

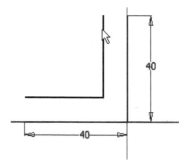

7. Click the **Line** button and draw lines closing the offset sketch.

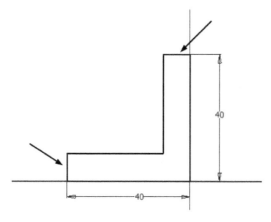

8. Add the offset dimension to the sketch.

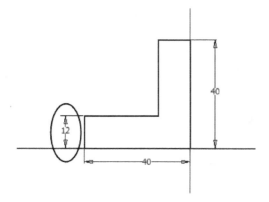

9. Click **Finish Sketch**.

10. Click **3D Model > Create > Extrude** on the ribbon.

11. Select the **Symmetric** option.

12. Set the **Distance** to 40 mm.

13. Click **OK** to create the first feature.

Creating the Shell feature
You can create a shell feature by removing a face of the model and applying thickness to other faces.

1. Click **3D Model > Modify > Shell** on the ribbon; the **Shell** dialog box appears.

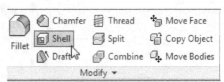

2. Set **Thickness** to 5 mm.

   Now, you need to select the faces to remove.

3. Select the top face and the back face of the model.

4. Select the front face and the bottom face of the model.

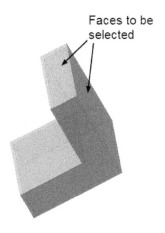

Faces to be selected

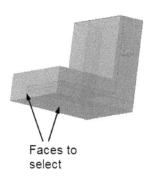

Faces to select

5.   Click OK to shell the model.

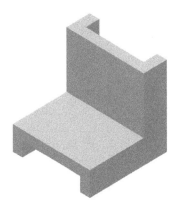

Creating the Third feature

1.   Click **3D Model > Sketch > Create 2D Sketch** on the ribbon.

2.   Select the front face of the model.

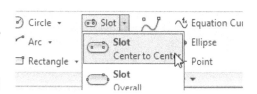

3.   Click **Sketch > Draw > Slot Center to Center** on the ribbon.

4.   Draw a slot by selecting the first, second, and third points.

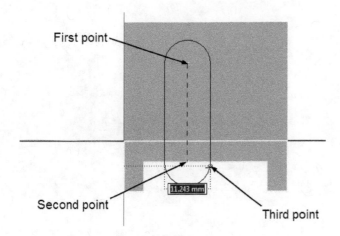

First point

Second point

Third point

11.243 mm

5.   Apply dimensions to the slot.

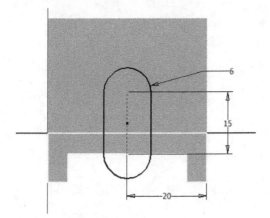

6

15

20

6.   Click **Finish Sketch**.

7.   Click **3D Model > Create > Extrude** on the ribbon.

8.   Select the sketch.

9.   Select the **To** option from the **Extents** drop-down.

10. Select the back face of the model.

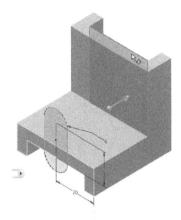

11. Click the **Join** button on the dialog box.

12. Click **OK** to create the feature.

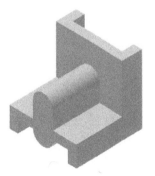

Creating a Cut Feature
1. Create the sketch on the front face of the model, as shown below.

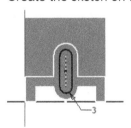

2. Finish the sketch.

3. Click **3D Model > Create > Extrude** on the ribbon.

4. Select the sketch.

5. Select the **All** option from the **Extents** drop-down.

6. Click the **Cut** button on the dialog box.

7. Click OK to create the cut feature.

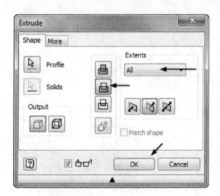

Creating the Rib Feature
In this section, you will create a rib feature at the middle of the model. To do so, you need to create a midplane.

1. To create a mid plane, click **3D Model > Work Features > Plane > Midplane between Two Parallel Planes** on the ribbon.

2. Select the right-face of the model.

3. Select the left face of the model; the midplane is created.

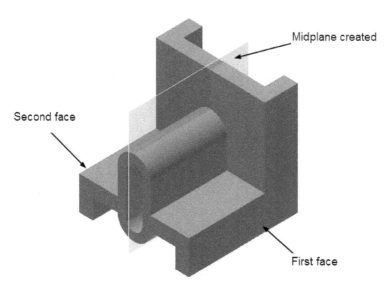

Midplane created

Second face

First face

4. Click **3D Model > Sketch > Create 2D Sketch** on the ribbon.

5. Select the mid plane.

6. Click the **Slice Graphics** button at the bottom of the window.

7. Click **Sketch > Draw > Project Geometry > Project Cut Edges** on the ribbon; the edges cut by the sketch plane are projected.

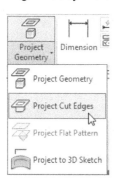

8. Draw the sketch, as shown below.

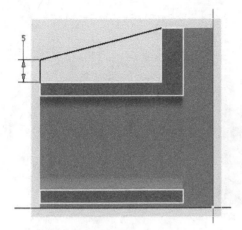

9. Finish the sketch.

10. Click **3D Model > Create > Rib** on the ribbon; the **Rib** dialog box appears.

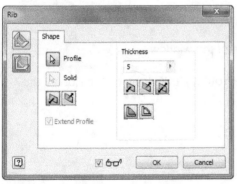

11. Select the sketch.

12. Click the **Parallel to Sketch** button on the dialog box.

13. Click the **Direction 1** button.

14. Set **Thickness** to 5 mm.

15. Click the **To Next** button.

16. Click the **Symmetric** button below the **Thickness** box.

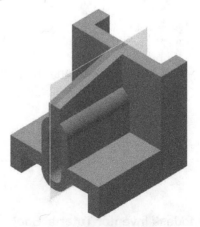

17. Click **OK** to create the rib feature.

18. To hide the midplane, select it and right-click.

Autodesk Inventor Tutorial Book

19. Click **Visibility** on the Marking Menu; the plane will be hidden.

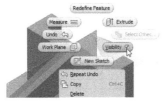

20. Save the Model.

TUTORIAL 3

In this tutorial, you will create a helical spring using the **Helix** and **Sweep along Guide** tools.

Creating the Coil

1. Open a new Inventor file using the **Standard (mm).ipt** template.

2. Create a sketch on the XZ plane.

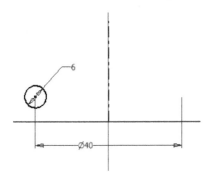

3. Finish the sketch.

4. To create a coil, click **3D Model > Create > Coil** on the ribbon; the **Coil** dialog box appears.

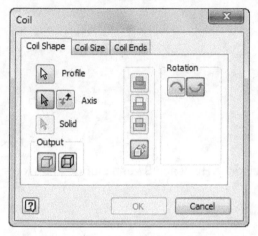

Also, the profile is automatically selected. Now, you need to select the axis of the coil.

5. Select the centerline as the axis.

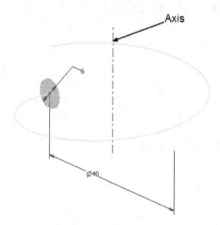

6. Click the **Coil Size** tab on the dialog box.

7. In the **Coil Size** tab, specify the settings as given next.

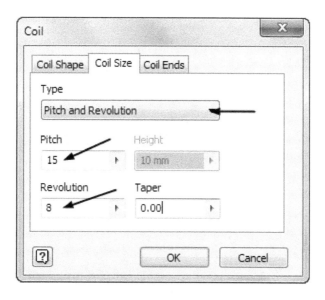

8. Click the **Coil Ends** tab on the dialog box.

9. Specify the settings in the **Coil Ends** tab as given next.

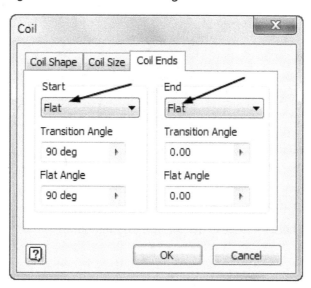

10. Click OK to create the coil.

14. Save the model a **Coil.ipt** and close the file.

TUTORIAL 4

In this tutorial, you create a shampoo bottle using the **loft**, **Extrude**, and **Thread** tools.

Creating First Section and Rails

To create a swept feature, you need to create sections and guide curves.

1. Open a new file in the Part modeling environment.

2. Click **3D Model > Sketch > Create 2D Sketch** on the ribbon.

3. Select the XY plane.

4. Click **Sketch > Draw > Ellipse** on the ribbon.

5. Draw the ellipse by selecting the points.

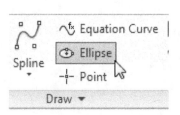

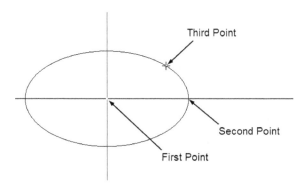

Third Point

Second Point

First Point

6. Add dimensions to the sketch.

7. Click **Finish Sketch**.

8. Click **3D Model > Sketch > Create 2D Sketch** on the ribbon.

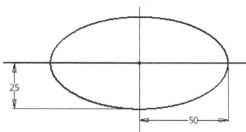

9. Select the XZ plane.

10. Click **Sketch > Draw > Spline > Spline Interpolation** on the ribbon.

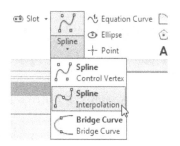

11. Create a spline similar to the one shown in figure.

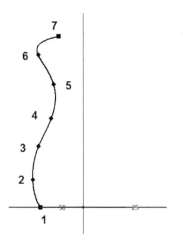

12. Apply Horizontal constraint between the first point of the spline and the origin point.

13. Draw a vertical construction line passing through the origin.

14. Apply dimension to the spline, as shown in figure.

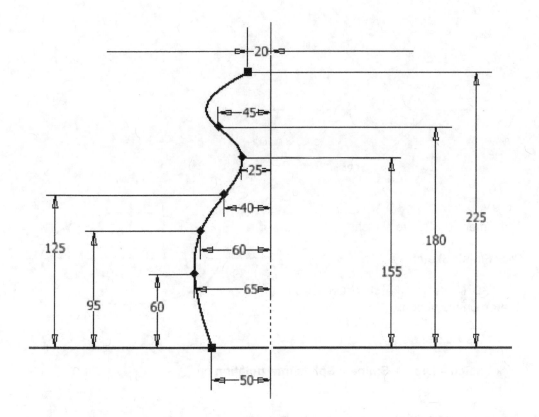

15. Click **Sketch > Pattern > Mirror** on the ribbon; the **Mirror** dialog box appears.

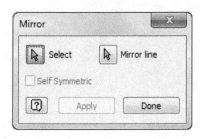

16. Select the spline.

17. Click **Mirror line** on the **Mirror** dialog box and then select the construction line.

18. Click **Apply** and then click **Done**.

19. Click **Finish Sketch**.

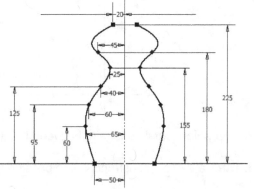

Creating the second section

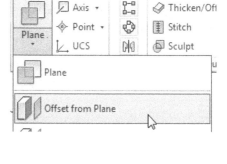

1. Click **3D Model > Work Features > Plane > Offset from Plane** on the ribbon.

2. Select the XZ plane from the Browser Bar.

3. Enter **225** in the **Distance** edit box.

4. Click OK.

5. Start a sketch on the newly created datum plane.

6. Create a circle of 40 mm diameter.

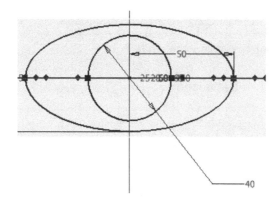

7. Click **Finish Sketch**.

Creating the Loft feature

1. To create a loft feature, click **3D Model > Create > Loft** on the ribbon; the **Loft** dialog box appears.

2. Select the **Rails** option on the dialog box.

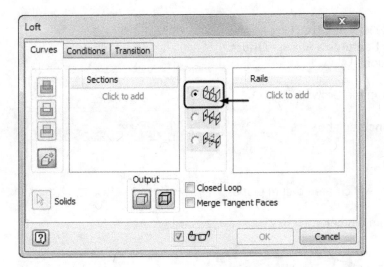

3. Click in the **Sections** group and select the circle.

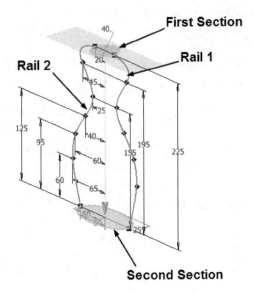

4. Select the ellipse.

5. Click in the **Rails** group.

6. Select the first rail.

7. Select the second rail.

8.   Click **OK** to create the loft feature.

Creating the Extruded feature

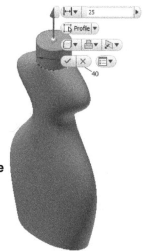

1.   Create a circle on the top of the sweep feature.

2.   Click the **Extrude** button on the **Create** panel.

3.   Extrude the circle upto 25 mm.

Creating the Emboss feature

1.   Click **3D Model > Work Features > Plane > Offset from Plane** on the ribbon.

2.   Select the XZ plane from the Browser Bar.

3.   Enter **50** in the **Distance** edit box.

4.   Create a sketch on the plane as shown in figure.

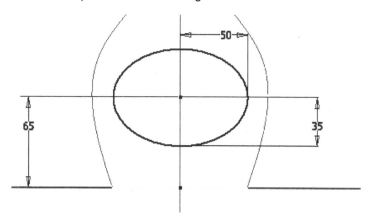

5.   Click **Finish Sketch**.

6.   Click **3D Model > Create > Emboss** on the ribbon; the **Emboss** dialog box appears.

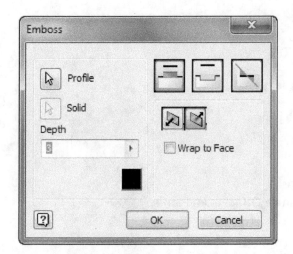

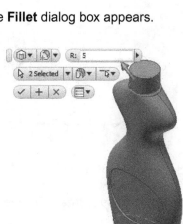

7. Click the **Engrave from Face** 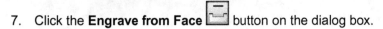 button on the dialog box.

8. Set the **Depth** to 3 mm.

9. Click **OK** to create the embossed feature.

Creating Fillets

1. Click **3D Model > Modify > Fillet** on the ribbon; the **Fillet** dialog box appears.

2. Click on the bottom and top edges of the swept feature.

3. Set **Radius** as 5 mm

4. Click **Click to add** on the dialog box.

5. Set **Radius** as 1 mm.

6. Select the edges of the emboss feature and click **OK**.

Shelling the Model

1. Click **3D Model > Modify > Shell** on the ribbon; the **Shell** dialog box appears.

2. Set **Thickness** as 1 mm.

3. Select the top face of the cylindrical feature.

4. Click **OK** to create the shell.

Creating Threads

1. Click **3D Model > Modify > Thread** on the ribbon; the **Thread** dialog box appears.

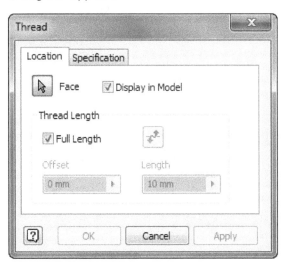

2. Clear the **Full Length** option.

3. Set the **Offset** and **Length** to 10 mm.

4. Select the cylindrical face.

5. Click the **Specification** tab.

6. Specify the following settings in this tab.

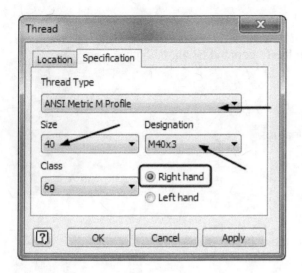

7. Click **OK** to create the thread.

8. Save the model and close it.

TUTORIAL 5
In this tutorial, you create a plastic basket.

Creating the Sweep Feature
To create a sweep feature, you need to draw a path and profile.

1. Click **3D Model > Sketch > Create 2D Sketch** on the ribbon.

2. Select the XY Plane from the **Browser Bar**.

3. Create a sketch as shown in figure.

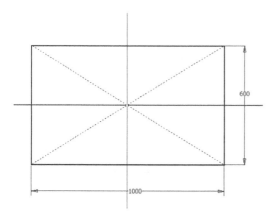

4. Click the **Fillet** button on the **Draw** panel; the **2D Fillet** dialog box appears.

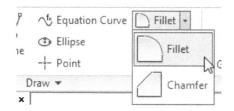

5. Enter **120** in the **2D Fillet** dialog box.

6. Select the lower horizontal line and right vertical line; a fillet is created at the corner.

7. Similarly, create fillets at all the other corners, as shown below.

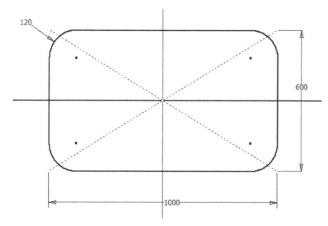

8. Click **Finish Sketch**.

    Creating the profile

9. Click **3D Model > Sketch > Create 2D Sketch** on the ribbon.

10. Select the YZ Plane from the **Browser Bar**.

11. Click the **Line** button on the **Draw** panel.

12. Select the start point and end point of the line, as shown in figure.

13. Press and drag the left mouse button to create a tangent arc, as shown in figure.

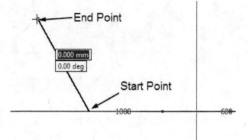

14. Create a horizontal construction line passing through the origin.

15. Add dimensions and constraints to the sketch as shown in figure.

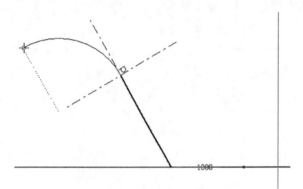

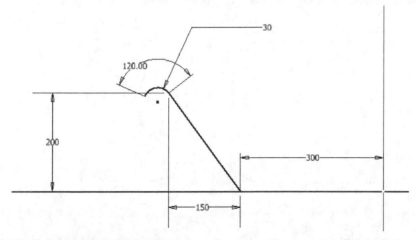

To display the applied constraints, click **Show All Constraints**  at the bottom of the window.

16. Finish the sketch.

17. Click **3D Model > Create > Sweep** on the ribbon; the **Sweep** dialog box appears.

18. Set the **Output** type to **Surface**.

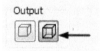

19. Click the **Profile** button on the dialog box.

20. Select the second sketch as the profile.

21. Select the first sketch as the path.

22. Click **OK** to create the swept surface.

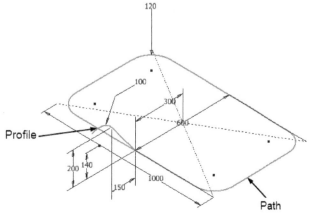

Creating the Patch Surface

1. To create a patch surface, click **3D Model > Surface > Patch** on the ribbon; the **Boundary Patch** dialog box appears.

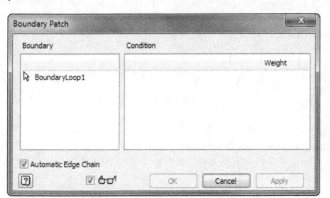

2. Make sure the **Automatic Edge Chain** option is selected.

☑ Automatic Edge Chain

3. Select the inner loop of the model.

4. Select **Free Condition** from the **Condition** group.

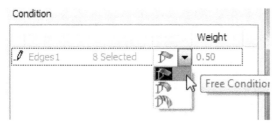

5.   Click **OK** to create the patch surface.

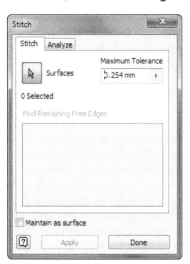

Stitching the Surfaces

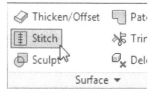

1.   To stitch the surface, click **3D Model > Surface > Stitch** on
     the ribbon; the **Stitch** dialog box appears .

2.   Select the swept surface and the patch surface.

3.   Accept the default settings and click **Apply**; the surfaces are stitched.

4.   Click **Done** to close the dialog box.

5.   Create a fillet **30** mm radius by selecting the inner edge loop.

Autodesk Inventor Tutorial Book

Adding Thickness to the surface

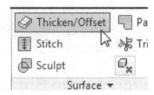

1. To add thickness to the surface model, click **3D Model > Surface > Thicken/ Offset** on the ribbon; the **Thicken/Offset** dialog box appears.

2. Select the **Quilt** option on the dialog box.

3. Set the **Distance** to **4** mm.

4. Select the surface.

5. Click **OK** to thicken the surface.

6. Right-click on the **Stitch Surface** in the **Browser Bar** and select **Visibility**; the surface is hidden.

Creating a Grill

A grill has openings or vents on a thin wall. To create a grill feature, first you need to create a sketch.

1. Click **3D Model > Sketch > Create 2D Sketch** on the ribbon.

2. Select the XZ Plane from the **Browser Bar**.

3. Click **Slice Graphics** at the bottom of the window; the model will be sliced by the sketching plane.

4. Create a sketch as shown below.

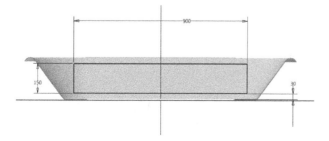

5. Click the **Rectangular Pattern** button on the **Pattern** panel.

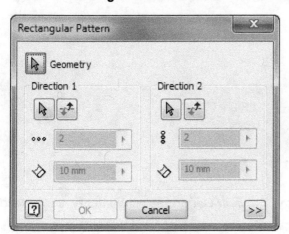

6. Select the left vertical line of the sketch.

7. Click the **Direction 1** button and select a horizontal line of the sketch; an arrow appears indicating the pattern direction.

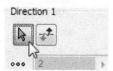

8. Click the **Flip** button to make sure the arrow points towards right.

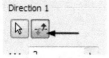

9. Set the **Count** to 19.

10. Set the **Spacing** to 50.

11. Click **OK** to create the pattern.

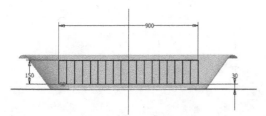

12. Click the **Rectangular Pattern** button.

13. Select the lower horizontal line.

14. Click the **Direction 1** button.

15. Select a horizontal line of the sketch.

16. Set the **Count** to 3 and **Spacing** to 50 mm.

17. Click **OK** to create the pattern.

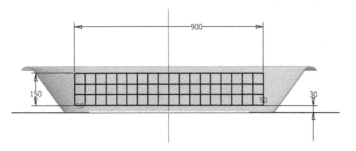

18. Right-click and select **Finish 2D Sketch**.

19. To create a grill, or click **3D Model > Plastic Part > Grill**; the **Grill** dialog box appears.

20. Select the boundary of the sketch.

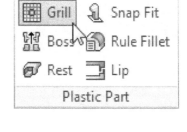

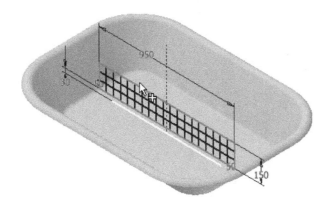

21. Set the parameters in the **Boundary** tab, as shown in figure.

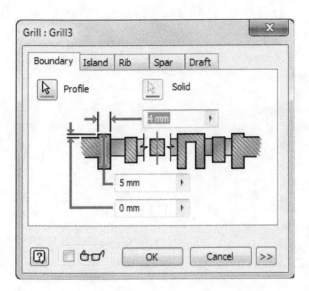

22. Click the **Rib** tab and select the vertical lines of the sketch.

23. Set the parameters in the **Rib** tab, as shown in figure.

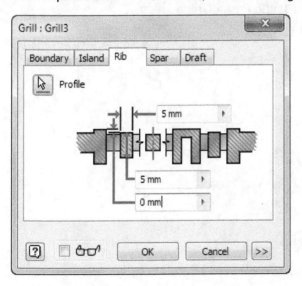

24. Click the **Spar** tab and select the vertical lines of the sketch.

25. Set the parameters in the **Spar** tab, as shown in figure.

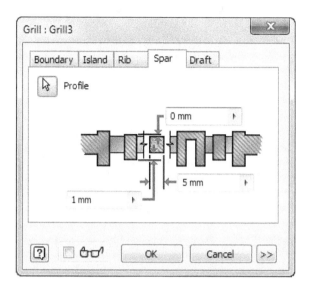

26. Click **OK** to create the grill feature.

27. Create a plane at a distance of 700 mm from the XZ Plane.

28. Copy the sketch of the grill feature from the **Browser Bar**.

29. Right-click on the newly created work plane and select **Paste**; the sketch is pasted on the work plane.

30. Use this sketch to create another grill feature, as shown below.

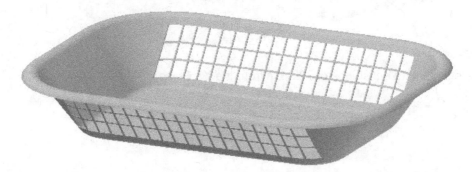

31. Create a sketch on the YZ Plane, as shown below.

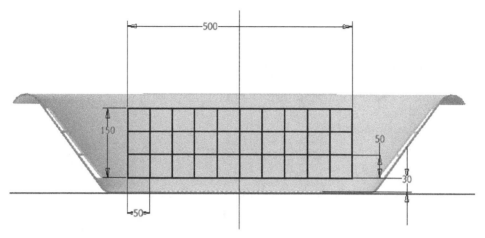

32. Create a grill feature on the left face, as shown below.

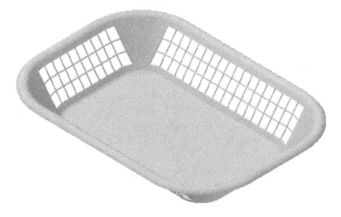

33. Similarly, create another grill feature on the right face.

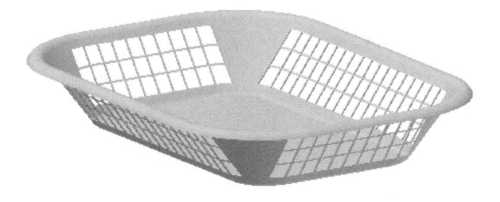

Applying a Rule Fillet

1. To apply a rule fillet, click **3D Model > Plastic Part > Rule Fillet** on the ribbon; the **Rule Fillet** dialog box appears.

2. Set the **Source** to **Feature** and **Radius** to 1 mm.

3. Select the **Rule** as **Against Part**.

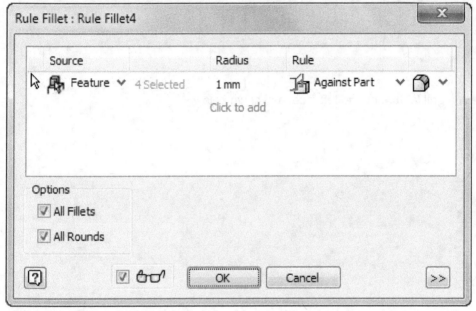

4. Select the grill feature from the model.

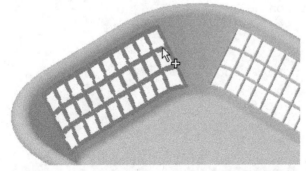

5. Similarly, select all the grill features and click **OK** to apply fillets to the grill features.

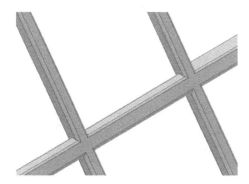

6. Save the model as **Plastic Basket.ipt** and close the file.

TUTORIAL 6

In this tutorial, you create a plastic casing.

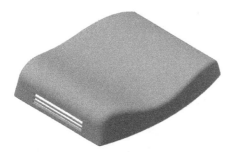

Creating the First Feature

1. Open a new Autodesk Inventor part file using the **Standard (mm).ipt** template.

2. Create a sketch on the XY Plane, as shown in figure.

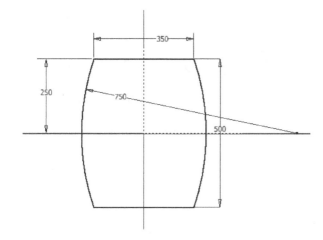

3.   Click **Finish Sketch**.

4.   Click the **3D Model > Create > Extrude** on the
     ribbon; the **Extrude** dialog box appears.

5.   Set the **Distance** to 80 mm.

6.   Click the **More** tab and set the **Taper** angle to -10.

7.   Click the **OK** button.

Creating the Extruded surface

1.   Click **3D Model > Sketch > Create 2D Sketch** on the ribbon and select the YZ Plane.

2.   Click the **Slice Graphics** button at the bottom of the or press **F7** on the keyboard.

3.   Click **Sketch > Draw > Spline > Spline Interpolation** on the ribbon.

4.   Create a spline as shown in figure.

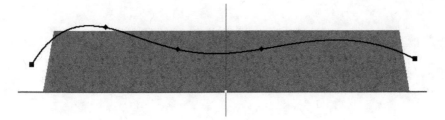

5.   Apply dimensions to the spline, as shown below.

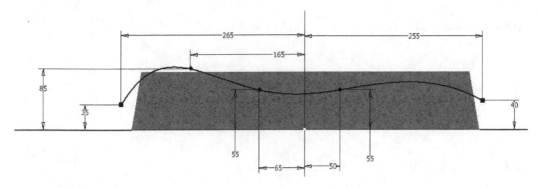

6.   Click **Finish Sketch**.

7.   Click the **Extrude** button.

8.   On the **Extrude** dialog box, set the **Output** type to **Surface**.

9. Set the **Extents** type to **Distance**.

10. Select the **Symmetric** button.

11. Extrude the sketch upto to 420 mm distance.

Replacing the top face of the model with the surface

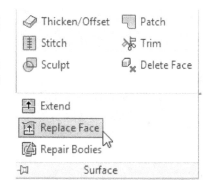

1. Expand the **Surface** panel on the **3D Model** ribbon and click the **Replace Face** button; the **Replace Face** dialog box appears.

Now, you need to select the face to be replaced.

2. Select the top face of the model.

Next, you need to select the replacement face or surface.

3. Click the **New Faces** button on the dialog box and select the extruded surface.

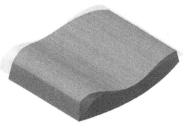

4. Click **OK** to replace the top face with a surface.

5. Hide the extruded surface.

Creating a Face fillet

1.   Click the **Fillet** button on the **Modify** panel.

2.   Click the **Face Fillet** button on the **Fillet** dialog box.

3.   Select the top surface as the first face and the inclined front face as the second face.

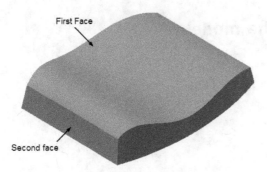

4.   Set the **Radius** to 40 mm and click the OK button to create the face fillet.

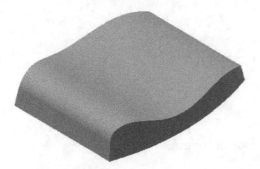

5.   Similarly, apply a face fillet of 30 mm radius between top surface and the back inclined face of the model.

Creating a Variable Radius fillet

1. Click the **Fillet** button on the **Modify** panel.

2. Click the **Variable** tab on the **Fillet** dialog box.

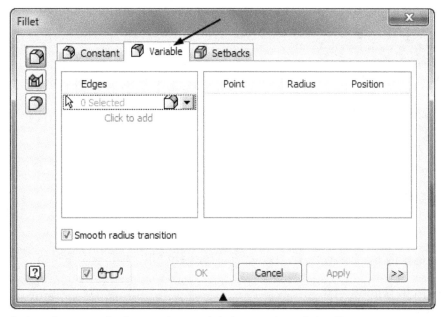

3. Select the curved edge on the model; the preview of the fillet appears.

4. Select a point on the fillet, as shown in figure.

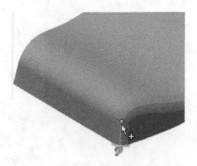

5.   Select another point the fillet, as shown in figure.

6.   Set the radii of the **Start**, **End**, **Point 1** and **Point 2** as shown below.

Point	Radius	Position
Start	15 mm	0.0
End	15 mm	1.0
Point 1	25 mm	0.2500 ul
Point 2	20 mm	0.6530 ul
	Click to add	

You can also specify the fillet type. By default, the **Tangent Fillet** type is specified.

7.   Select **Smooth (G2) Fillet** type.

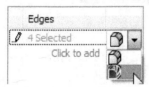

8.   Make sure the **Smooth radius transition** option is selected.

9.   Click OK to create the variable fillet.

Mirroring the fillet

10. Click the **Mirror** button on the **Pattern** panel; the **Mirror** dialog box appears.

11. Select the variable radius fillet from the model.

12. Click the **Mirror Plane** button on the dialog box.

13. Select the **YZ Plane** from the Browser Bar.

14. Click **OK** to mirror the fillet.

Shelling the Model
1. Click the **Shell** button on the **Modify** panel; the **Shell** dialog box appears.

2. Click the **Inside** button on the dialog box and set the **Thickness** to 5 mm.

3. Rotate the model and select the bottom face.

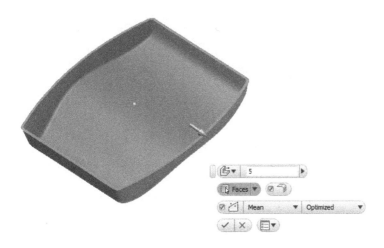

4.   Click OK.

Creating the Boss Features

1. Click **3D Model > Sketch > Create 2D Sketch** on the
    ribbon and select the bottom face of the model.

2. Draw a rectangle with **Construction** button selected
    on the **Format** panel.

3. Apply dimensions to the rectangle.

4. Click the **Point** button on the **Draw** panel.

5. Place four points at corners of the rectangle.

6. Click **Finish Sketch**.

Now, you will create bosses by selecting the points created in the sketch.

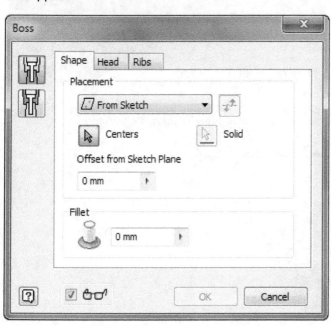

7. Click the **Boss** button on the **Plastic Part** panel; the **Boss** dialog
    box appears.

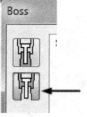

8. Click the **Thread** button on the dialog box.

9. Select the **From Sketch** option from the **Placement** group.

10. Select the points located on the corners of the rectangle; the bosses are placed at the selected points.

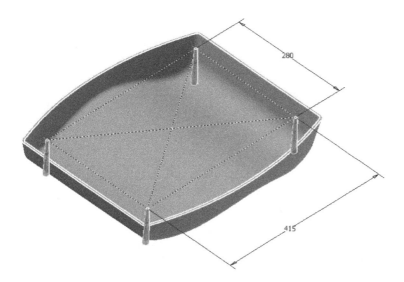

11. Click the **Thread** tab and specify the parameters as shown below.

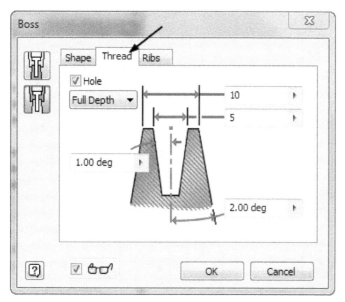

12. Click the **Ribs** tab and select the **Stiffening Ribs** option.

13. Set the rib parameters as shown below.

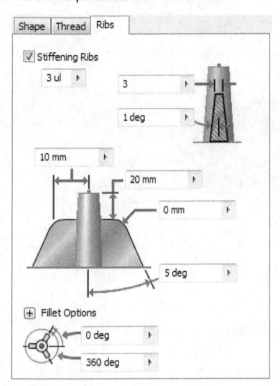

14. Expand the **Fillet options**.

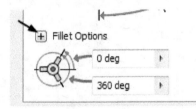

15. Specify the fillet options as shown below.

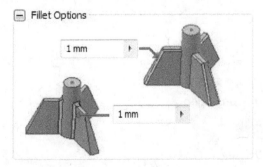

16. Click OK to create the bosses with ribs.

Creating the Lip feature

1. Click the **Lip** button on the **Plastic Part** panel of the ribbon; the **Lip** dialog box appears.

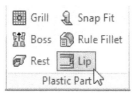

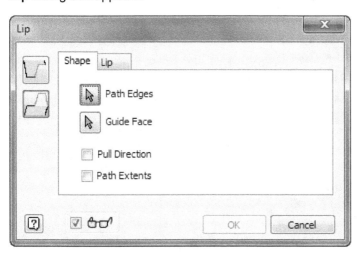

2. Click the **Lip** button on the dialog box.

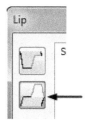

3. Select the outer edge of the bottom face.

4. Click the **Guide Face** button on the dialog box and select the bottom face of the model.

5. Click the **Lip** tab and set the parameters as shown below.

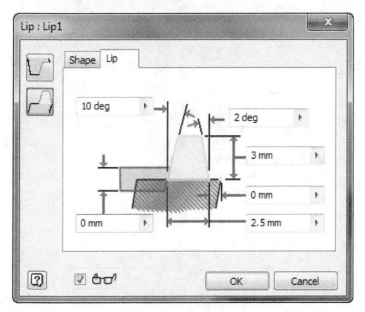

6.   Click OK to create the lip.

Creating the Grill Feature

1.   Create a sketch on the front inclined face.

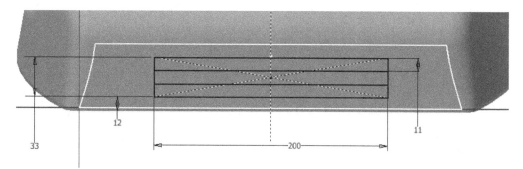

2.   Click the **Grill** button on the **Plastic Part** panel.

3.   Select the rectangle as the boundary and set the **Boundary** parameters as shown below.

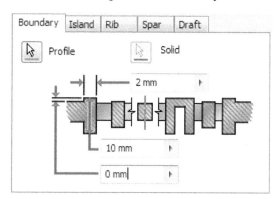

4.   Click the **Rib** tab and select the horizontal lines.

Autodesk Inventor Tutorial Book

5. Set the rib parameters as shown below.

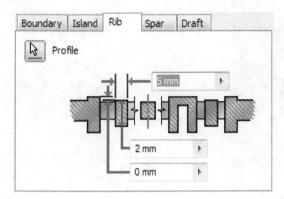

6. Click **OK** to create the grill.

7. Save the model as Plastic Cover.ipt and close it.

6. Sheet Metal Modeling

This Chapter will show you to:

- *Create Face feature*
- *Create Flange*
- *Create Contour Flange*
- *Create Corner Seam*
- *Create Punches*
- *Create Bend Feature*
- *Create Corner Rounds*
- *Flat Pattern*

TUTORIAL 1

In this tutorial, you create the sheet metal model shown in figure.

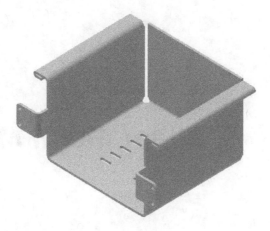

Creating a New Sheet metal File

1. To create a new sheet metal file, click the **New** button on the **Get Started** ribbon; the **Create New File** dialog box appears.

2. Click **Sheet Metal (mm).ipt**.

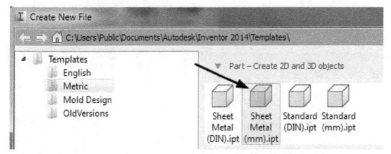

3. Click **Create**; a new Autodesk Inventor Sheet metal window appears.

Setting the Parameters of the Sheet Metal part

1. To set the parameters, click **Sheet Metal > Setup > Sheet Metal Defaults** on the ribbon; the **Sheet Metal Defaults** dialog box appears.

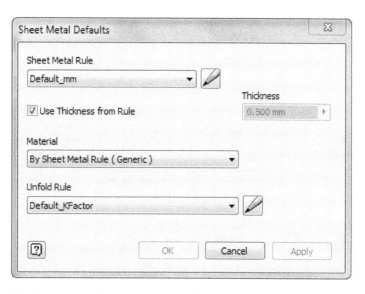

This dialog box displays the default preferences of the sheet metal part such as sheet metal rule, thickness, material, and unfold rule. You can change these preferences as per you requirement.

2.   To edit the sheet metal rule, click the **Edit Sheet Metal Rule** button on the dialog box; the **Style and Standard Editor** dialog box appears.

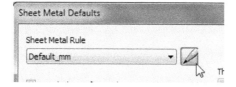

In the **Sheet** tab of this dialog box, you can set the sheet preferences such as sheet thickness, material, flat pattern bend angle representation, flat pattern punch representation and gap size.

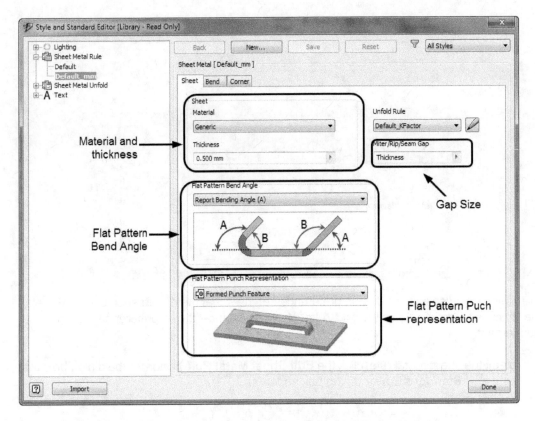

3. In the **Sheet** tab, set the Thickness to 3 mm and leave all the default settings.

4. Click the **Bend** tab.

In the **Bend** tab of this dialog box, you can set the bend preferences such as bend radius, bend relief shape and size, and bend transition.

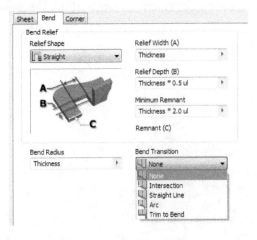

5. Set the **Relief Shape** to **Round**.

6. Click the **Corner** tab.

In the **Corner** tab, you can set the shape and size of the corner relief to be applied at the corners.

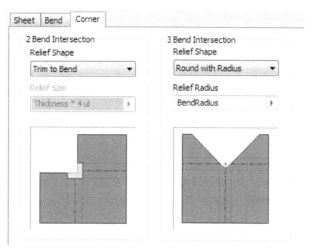

7. After setting the required preferences, click the **Done** button on the dialog box and then click **Yes**.

The Unfold Rule defines the folding/unfolding method of the sheetmetal part. To modify or set a new Unfold Rule, click the **Edit Unfold Rule** button on the **Sheet Metal Defaults** dialog box.

On the **Style and Standard Editor** dialog box, select the required **Unfold Method**.

You can define the Unfold rule by selecting the Linear method (specifying the K factor), selecting a Bend Table, or entering a custom equation. Click **Done** after settings the parameters.

Creating the Base Feature
1. Create the sketch on the XY Plane, as shown in figure.

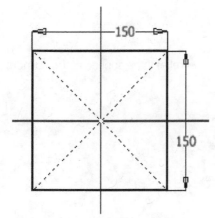

2. Click **Finish Sketch**.

3. To create the base component, click **Sheet Metal > Create > Face** on the ribbon; the **Face** dialog box appears.

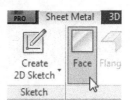

4. Click **OK** to create the tab feature.

Creating the flange

1. To create the flange, click **Sheet Metal > Create > Flange** on the ribbon; the **Flange** dialog box appears.

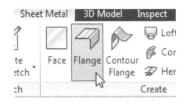

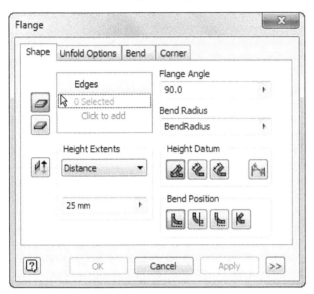

2. Select the edge on the top face.

3. Set the **Distance** to 100.

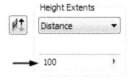

4. Click OK to create the flange.

Creating the Contour Flange

1. Draw a sketch on the front face of the flange, as shown in figure.

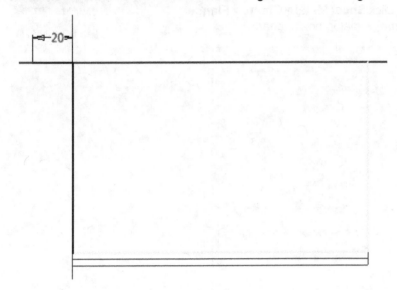

2. Click **Finish Sketch**.

3. To create the contour flange, click **Sheet Metal > Create > Contour Flange** on the ribbon; the **Contour Flange** dialog box appears.

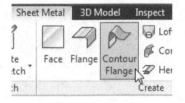

4.   Select the sketch from the model.

5.   Select the edge on the left side of the top face; the contour flange preview appears.

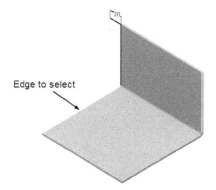
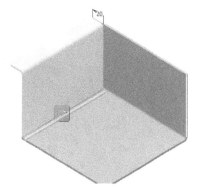

6.   Click >> located at the bottom of the dialog box.

7.   Select **Edge** from the Width **Type** drop-down.

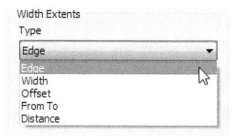

8.   Click **OK** to create the contour flange.

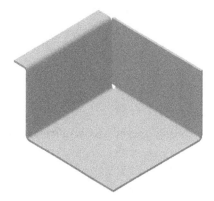

Creating the Corner Seam

1.   To create the corner seam, click **Sheet Metal> Modify > Corner Seam** on the ribbon; the **Corner Seam** dialog box appears.

Autodesk Inventor Tutorial Book

2. Rotate the model.

3. Select the two edges forming the corner.

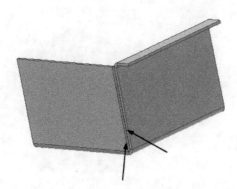

4. Set the parameters in the **Shape** tab of the dialog box.

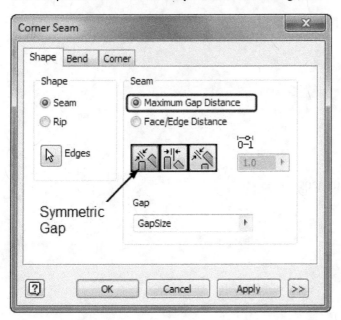

5. Click the **Bend** tab and make sure that the **Default** option is selected in the **Bend Transition** drop-down.

6. Click the **Corner** tab and set the **Relief Shape** to **Round**.

    You can also apply other type of relief using the options in the **Relief Shape** drop-down.

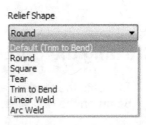

Creating a Sheet Metal Punch iFeature

1. Open a new sheet metal file using the **Sheet Metal (mm).ipt** template.

2. Create a sheet metal face of the dimensions 100x100 mm.

3. Click **Manage > Parameters > Parameters** on the ribbon; the **Parameters** dialog box appears.

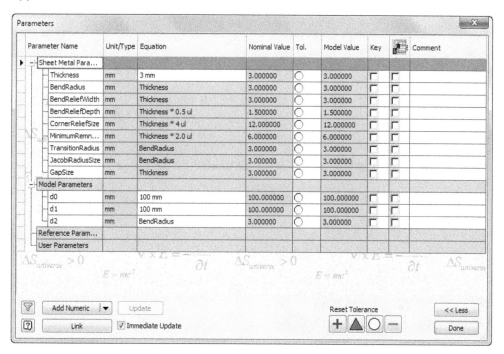

4. Select the **User Parameters** row and click the **Add Numeric** button on the dialog box; a new row is added.

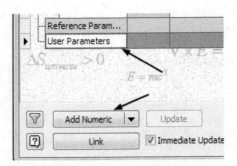

5.   Enter **Diameter** in the new row.

6.   Set **Unit Type** to **mm** and **Equation** to **1 mm**.

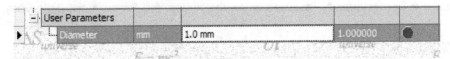

7.   Similarly, create a parameter named **Length** and specify its values as shown below.

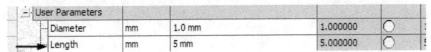

8.   Click **Done**.

9.   Click **Sheet Metal > Sheet Metal > Create 2D Sketch** on the ribbon.

10. Select the top face of the base feature.

11. Draw a slot, as shown in figure.

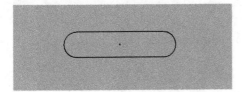

12. Click **Dimension** on the **Constrain** panel and select the round end of the slot.

13. Click to display the **Edit Dimension** box.

14. Click the arrow button on the box and select **List Parameters** from the shortcut menu; the **Parameters** list appears.

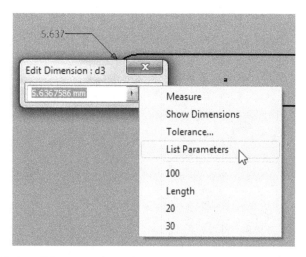

15. Select **Diameter** from the list and click the green check on the **Edit Dimension** box.

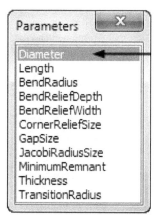

16. Similarly, dimension the horizontal line of the slot and set the parameter to **Length**.

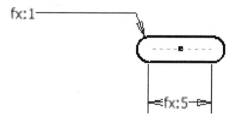

17. Click the **Point** button on the **Draw** panel and place it at the center of the slot.

18. Delete the projected edges (yellow lines) from the sketch.

19. Click **Finish Sketch**.

20. Click **Sheet Metal > Modify > Cut** on the ribbon; the **Cut** dialog box appears.

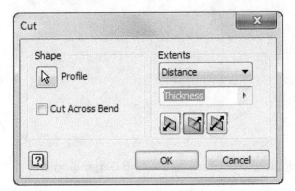

21. Accept the default values and click **OK** to create the cut feature.

22. Click **Manage > Author > Extract iFeature** on the ribbon; the **Extract iFeature** dialog box appears.

23. In the dialog box, set the **Type** to **Sheet Metal Punch iFeature**.

24. Select the cut feature from the model or from the Browser Bar; the parameters of the cut feature appear in the **Extract iFeature** dialog box.

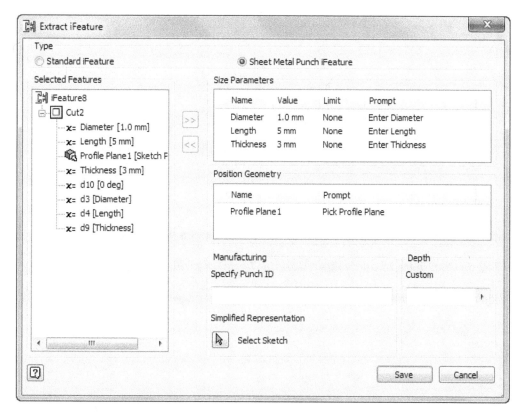

Next, you need to set the **Size Parameters** of the iFeature.

25. Set the **Limit** of the **Diameter** value to **Range**; the **Specify Range** dialog box appears.

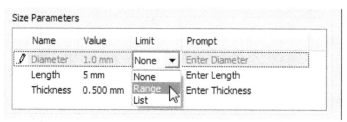

26. Set the values in the **Specify Range** dialog box, as shown below and click **OK**.

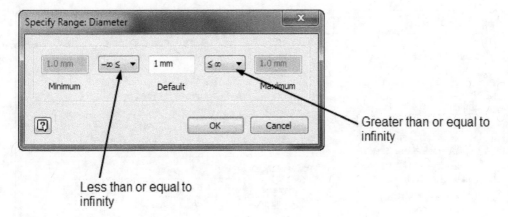

27. Set the **Limit** of the **Length** value to **List**; the **List Values** dialog box appears.

28. Click on **Click here to add value** and enter **7** mm as value.

29. Similarly, specify the values in the **List** dialog box, as shown below.

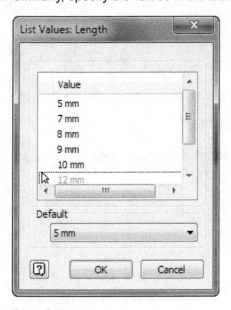

30. Click **OK**.

31. Set the **Limit** of the **Thickness** value to **Range**; the **Specify Range** dialog box appears.

32. Set the values in the **Specify Range** dialog box, as shown below. Next, click OK.

Next, you need to select the center point of the slot. This point will be used while placing the slot.

33. Click the **Select Sketch** button on the **Extract iFeature** dialog box.

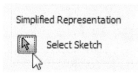

34. Select the sketch of the cut feature from the Browser Bar.

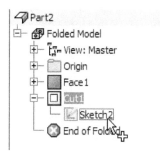

35. Click **Save**; the **Save As** dialog box appears.

36. Browse to the **Punches** folder and enter **Custom slot** in the **File name** field.

37. Click **Save**.

38. Click **Application Menu > Save**.

39. Save the sheet metal part file as **Custom slot**.

40. Switch to the sheet metal file of the current tutorial.

Creating a Punched feature

1. Create a sketch on the top face of the base feature, as shown below.

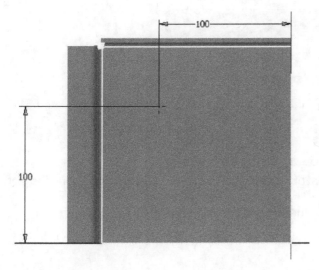

2.   Click **Finish Sketch**.

3.   To create the punch, click **Sheet Metal > Modify > Punch Tool** on the ribbon; the **PunchTool Directory** dialog box appears.

4.   Select **Custom slot.ide** from the dialog box and click **Open**; the **PunchTool** dialog box appears .

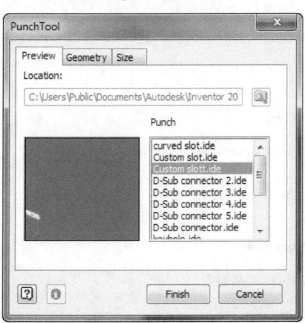

5.   Click the **Size** tab on the **PunchTool** dialog box.

6.   Set **Length** to **12** and **Diameter** to **2**.

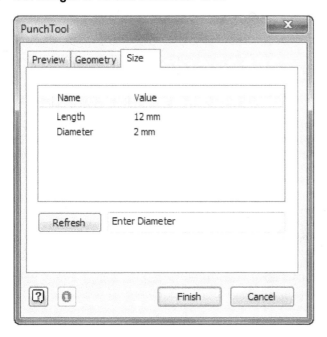

7.   Click **Refresh** to preview the slot.

8.   Click **Finish** to create the slot.

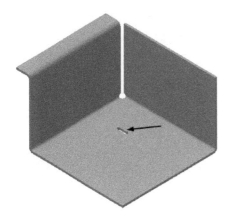

Creating the Rectangular Pattern

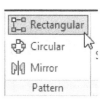

1.   Click **Sheet Metal > Pattern > Rectangular Pattern** on the ribbon; the **Rectangular Pattern** dialog box appears.

2.   Select the slot feature.

3. Click the **Direction 1** button on the dialog box.

4. Select the edge of the base feature as shown below.

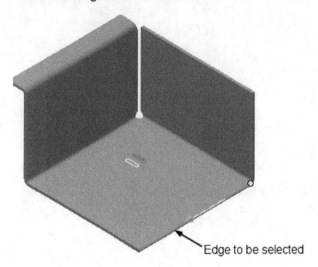

Edge to be selected

5. Select **Spacing** from the drop-down located in the **Direction 1** group.

6. Specify **Column Count** as 5.

7. Specify **Column Span** as 15.

8. Click the **Direction 2** button on the dialog box.

9. Select the edge on the base feature, as shown below.

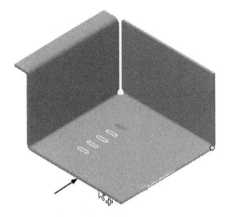

10. Click the **Flip** button to make sure the arrow is pointed toward right.

11. Select **Spacing** from the drop-down located in the **Direction 2** group.

12. Specify **Column Count** as 2.

13. Specify **Column Span** as 50.

14. Click **OK** to create the pattern.

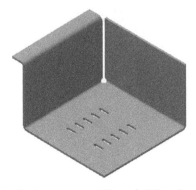

Autodesk Inventor Tutorial Book

Creating the Bend Feature

1. Create a plane parallel to the front face of the flange feature. The offset distance is 160 mm.

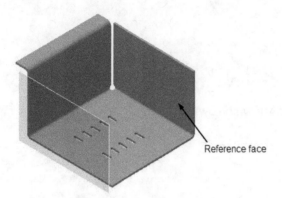

Reference face

2. Create a sketch on the new work plane.

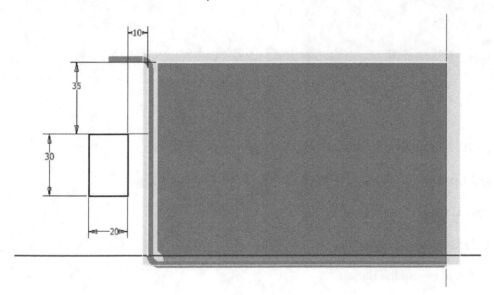

3. Click **Sheet Metal > Create > Face** on the ribbon and create a face feature.

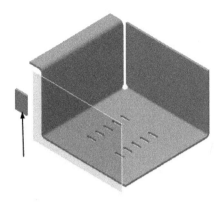

4. Click **Sheet Metal > Create > Bend** on the ribbon; the **Bend** dialog box appears.

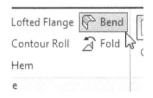

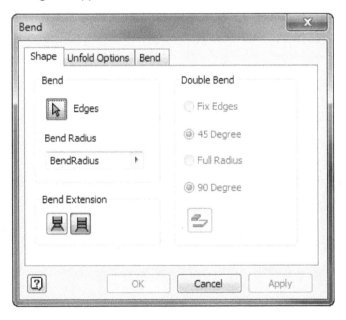

5. Select the edges from the model as shown below.

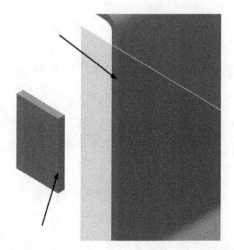

6.   Make sure the **Bend Extension** is set to perpendicular.

7.   Click **OK** to create the bend feature.

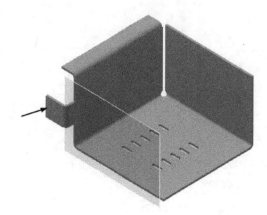

8.   Hide the work plane.

Applying a corner round

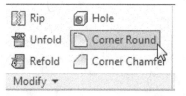

1.   To apply a corner round, click **Sheet Metal > Modify > Corner Round** on the ribbon; the **Corner Round** dialog box appears.

2.   Set **Radius** as 5.

3.   Set the **Select Mode** to **Feature**.

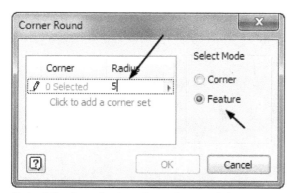

4.   Select the face feature from the model.

5.   Click **OK** to apply the rounds.

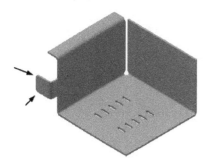

Creating Countersink holes

1.   Click **Sheet Metal > Modify > Hole** on the ribbon; the **Hole** dialog box appears.

2.   Set the **Placement** method to **Concentric**.

3.   Set the hole type to **Countersink**.

Autodesk Inventor Tutorial Book

4. Set the other parameters on the dialog box, as shown below.

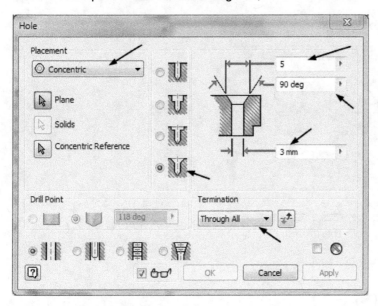

5. Click on the face of the flange, as shown below.

6. Select the corner round as the concentric reference.

7. Click Apply.

8. Again click on the flange face and select the other corner round as the concentric reference.

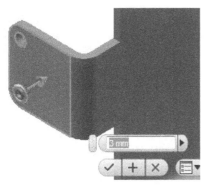

9. Click **OK** to create the countersink holes.

Creating Hem features

1. To create the hem feature, click **Sheet Metal > Create > Hem** on the ribbon; the **Hem** dialog box appears.

2. Set the **Type** to **Single**.

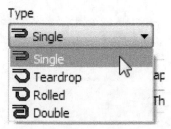

3. Select the edge of the contour flange, as shown below.

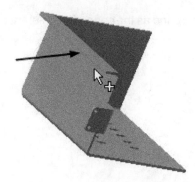

4. Leave the default settings of the dialog box and click **OK** to create the hem.

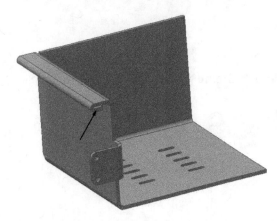

Mirroring the Features

1. Click **Mirror** on the **Pattern** panel; the **Mirror** dialog box appears.

2. Click >> at the bottom of the dialog box and make sure the **Creation Method** is set to **Identical**.

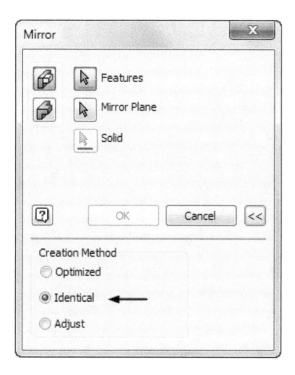

3. Select the features from the **Browser Bar**, as shown below.

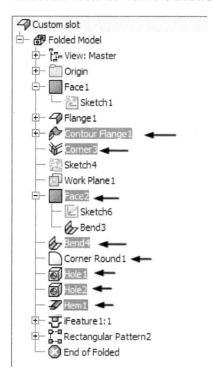

4. Click the **Mirror Plane** button on the dialog box and select the **YZ Plane** from the Browser Bar.

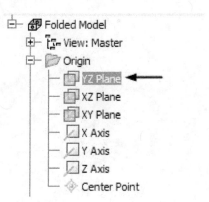

5. Click OK to mirror the feature.

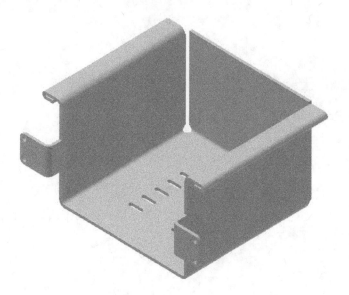

Creating the Flat Pattern

1. To create a flat pattern, click **Sheet Metal > Flat Pattern > Flat Pattern** on the ribbon.

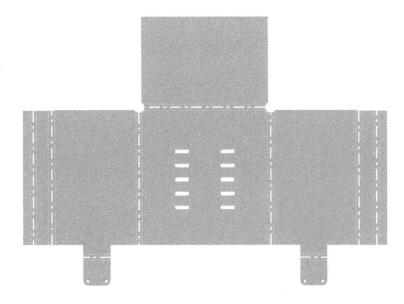

You can set order in which the bends will be annotation.

2. Click the **Bend Order Annotation** button on the **Manage** panel; the order in which the bends will be annotated is displayed .

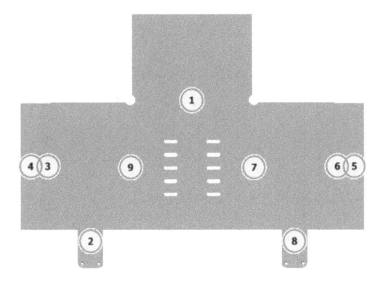

3. To change the order of the bend annotation, click on the center line of the bend; the **Bend Order Edit** dialog box appears.

4. Select the **Bend Number** check box and enter a new number in the edit box.

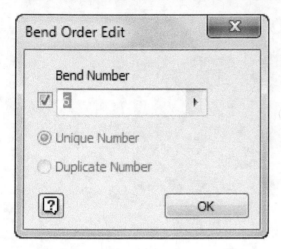

5. Click **OK** to change the order.

6. To switch back to the folded view of the model, click **Go to Folded Part** on the **Folded Part** panel.

7. Save the sheet metal part and close.

7. Assembly Modeling Tools

In this chapter, you will learn to

- *Create a top-down assembly*
- *Create assembly joints*

TUTORIAL 1

In this tutorial, you create the model shown in figure. You use top-down assembly approach to create this model.

Creating a New Assembly File

1. To create a new assembly, click **Get Started > Launch > New** on the ribbon; the **Create New File** dialog box appears.

2. Click **Standard (mm).iam** in the **Assembly- Assemble 2D and 3D components** group.

3. Click **Create**; a new Inventor assembly window appears.

Creating a component in the Assembly

In a top-down assembly approach, you create components of an assembly directly in the assembly by using the **Create** tool.

1. Click **Create** on the **Component** panel; the **Create In-Place Component** dialog box appears.

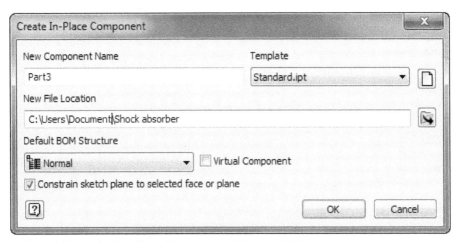

2. Enter **Shock Base** in the **New Component Name** field.

3. Click the **Browse Templates** button on the dialog box; the **Open Templates** dialog box appears.

4. Click the **Metric** tab on the **Open Template** dialog box and select **Standard (mm).ipt**.

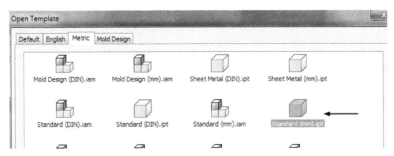

5. Click **OK.**

6. In the **Create In-Place Component** dialog box, set the **New File Location** to C:/Document/Shock absorber.

7. Click **OK**.

8. Expand the **Origin** in **Browser Bar** and select the **XY Plane**; the **3D Model** tab is activated in the ribbon.

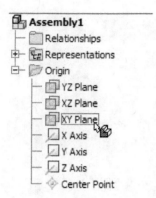

9. Click **Sketch > Create 2D Sketch** on the ribbon.

10. Select **YZ Plane**.

11. Create a sketch as shown below.

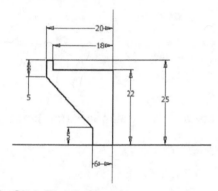

12. Click **Finish Sketch**.

13. Click **3D Model > Create > Revolve** on the ribbon and create a revolved feature as shown below.

14. Create a through hole of 6 mm diameter.

Return

15. Click **Return** on the ribbon; the **Assemble** tab is activated.

Creating the Second Component of the Assembly

1. Click **Assemble > Component > Create** on the ribbon; the **Create In-Place Component** dialog box appears.

2. Enter **Shock Connector** in the **New Component name** field.

3. Click the **Browse Templates** button on the dialog box; the **Open Templates** dialog box appears.

4. Click the **Metric** tab on the **Open Template** dialog box and select **Standard (mm).ipt**.

5. Click **OK.**

6. In the **Create In-Place Component** dialog box, set the **New File Location** to C:/Document/Shock absorber.

7. Select **Constrain sketch plane to select face or plane** option.

8. Click OK.

9. Select the bottom face of the Shock Base.

10. Click **Sketch > Create 2D Sketch** on the ribbon.

11. Select **XY Plane**.

12. Create a sketch as shown below.

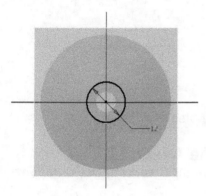

13. Click **Finish Sketch**.

14. Extrude the sketch upto 10 mm distance.

15. Create a sketch on the YZ Plane as shown below.

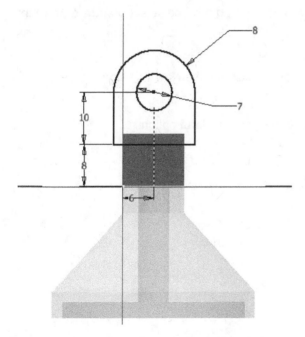

16. Extrude the sketch symmetrically upto 6 mm distance.

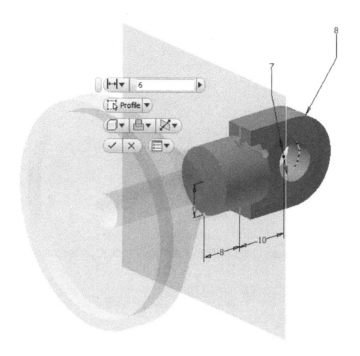

17. Create a hole of 6 mm diameter and 6 mm depth on the top face of the first feature.

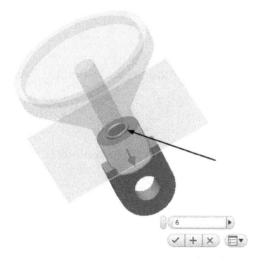

18. Click **Return** on the ribbon.

Applying Constraints between the two components

1.   Click **Constrain** on the **Relationships** panel.

2. Click the **Mate** button on the **Place Constraint** dialog box.

3. Align the axes of the two parts.

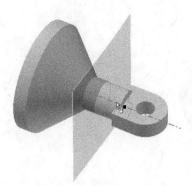 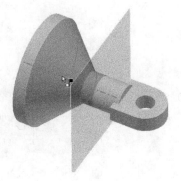

4. Next, apply the **Mate** constraint between the **YZ Plane** of the Shock Connector and the **YZ Plane** of the Shock Base.

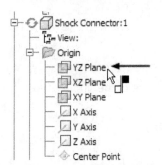 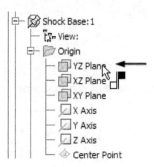

Creating the third Component

1. Click **Assemble > Component > Create** on the ribbon; the **Create In-Place Component** dialog box appears.

2. Enter **Rod** in the **New Component name** field.

3. Click the **Browse Templates** button on the dialog box; the **Open Templates** dialog box appears.

4. Click the **Metric** tab on the **Open Template** dialog box and select **Standard (mm).ipt**.

5. Click **OK.**

6. In the **Create In-Place Component** dialog box, set the **New File Location** to C:/Document/Shock absorber.

7. Select **Constrain sketch plane to select face or plane** option.

8. Click **OK**.

9. Select the XZ Plane from the Browser Bar.

10. Click **Sketch > Create 2D Sketch** on the ribbon.

11. Expand origin under Rod and select **XY Plane**.

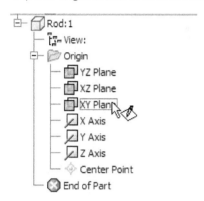

12. Create a rectangular sketch as shown below.

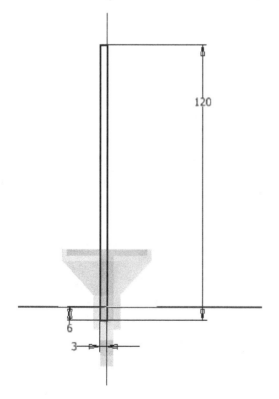

13. Click **Finish Sketch**.

14. Revolve the sketch.

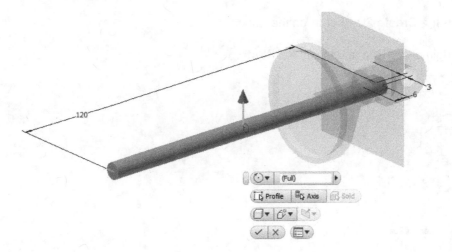

15. Click **Return** on the ribbon.

Constraining the Rod

1.   Hide the Shock Base (Right-click on it and select **Visibility**).

2.   Move the Rod by dragging it.

3.   Click **Constrain** on the **Relationships** panel.

4.   Click the **Insert** button on the **Place Constraint** dialog box.

5.   Select the bottom edge of the Rod and then select the bottom edge of the hole in the Shock Connector.

   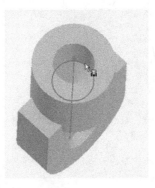

6.   Click OK.

Creating the fourth Component

1. Click **Assemble > Component > Create** on the ribbon; the **Create In-Place Component** dialog box appears.

2. Enter **Cylinder** in the **New Component name** field.

3. Click the **Browse Templates** button on the dialog box; the **Open Templates** dialog box appears.

4. Click the **Metric** tab on the **Open Template** dialog box and select **Standard (mm).ipt**.

5. Click **OK.**

6. In the **Create In-Place Component** dialog box, set the **New File Location** to C:/Document/Shock absorber.

7. Select **Constrain sketch plane to select face or plane** option.

8. Click **OK**.

9. Select the XZ Plane from the Browser Bar.

10. Click **Sketch > Create 2D Sketch** on the ribbon.

11. Expand origin under Cylinder and select **XY Plane**.

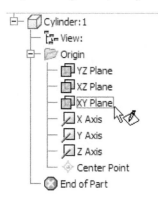

12. Create a sketch as shown below.

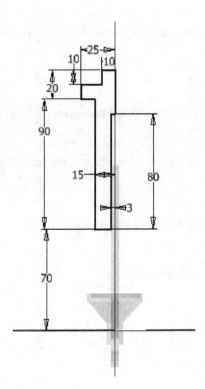

13. Revolve the sketch.

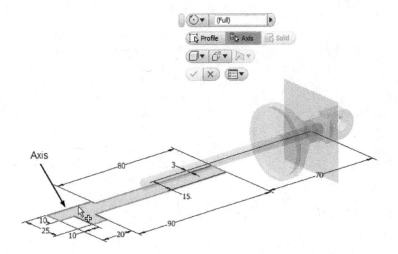

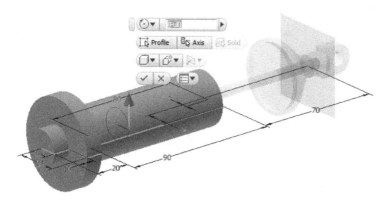

14. Create a sketch on the YZ Plane of the Cylinder.

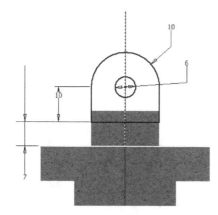

15. Extrude the sketch symmetrically upto 10 mm.

16. Click **Return** to return to the assembly.

Autodesk Inventor Tutorial Book

Constraining the Cylinder

1.   Move the Cylinder by dragging it.

2.   Click **Constrain** on the **Relationships** panel.

3.   Click the **Mate** button on the **Place Constraint** dialog box.

4.   Align the axes of the Cylinder and Rod.

5.   Click Apply.

6.   Apply the Mate constraint between the faces of the cylinder and the Shock Base.

7.   Enter **138** in the **Offset** box.

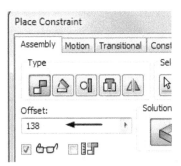

Creating the fifth Component

1.   Click **Assemble > Component > Create** on the ribbon; the **Create In-Place Component** dialog box appears.

2.   Enter **Spring** in the **New Component name** field.

3.   Click the **Browse Templates** button on the dialog box; the **Open Templates** dialog box appears.

4.   Click the **Metric** tab on the **Open Template** dialog box and select **Standard (mm).ipt**.

5.   Click **OK.**

6.   In the **Create In-Place Component** dialog box, set the **New File Location** to C:/Document/Shock absorber.

7. Select **Constrain sketch plane to select face or plane** option.

8. Click **OK**.

9. Select the top face of the Shock Base.

10. Click **Sketch > Create 2D Sketch** on the ribbon.

11. Select the top face of the Shock Base.

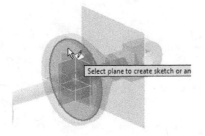

12. Create a sketch as shown below.

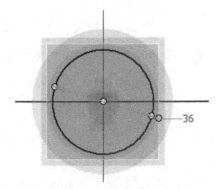

13. Extrude the sketch upto 138 mm distance.

14. Click **Sketch > Create 2D Sketch** on the ribbon.

15. Click **Slice Graphics** at the bottom of the window.

16. Create the sketch as shown below (draw a center line and a circle).

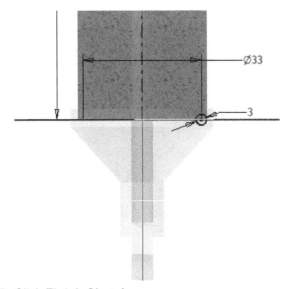

17. Click **Finish Sketch**.

18. Click **3D Model > Create > Coil** on the ribbon.

19. Select the centerline of the sketch to define the axis of the coil.

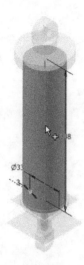

20. Click the **Intersect** button on the **Coil** dialog box.

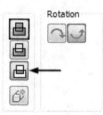

21. Click the **Coil Size** tab.

22. Set the **Type** to **Pitch and Height**.

23. Set the **Height** to 138.

24. Set the **Pitch** to 138/10.

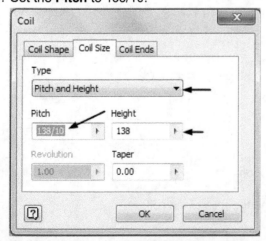

25. Click OK to create the coil.

26. Click **Return** to return to the assembly.

Constraining the Spring

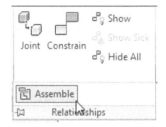

1. Click the **Assemble** button on the **Relationships** panel.

2. Select **Mate - Mate** from the Mini toolbar.

3. Select the Z axis of the Spring and then the Z axis of the Assembly.

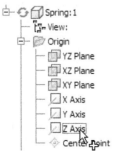

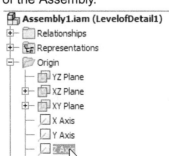

4. Click OK.

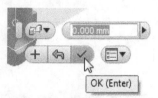

5. Similarly, apply the mate constraint between the YZ Plane of the Spring and the YZ Plane of the Assembly.

6. Save the assembly and all its parts.

TUTORIAL 2

In this tutorial, you create a slider crank mechanism by applying Joints.

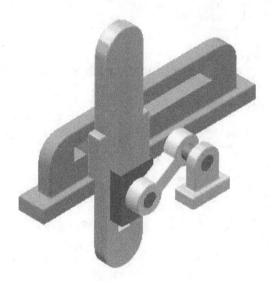

1. Download the part files of the assembly from the companion website. Next, save the files in the **Slider Crank Assembly** folder.

2. Start a new assembly file using the **Standard (mm).iam** template.

3. Click **Assemble > Component > Place** on the ribbon.

4. Browse to the **Slider Crank Assembly** folder and double-click on **Base**.

5. Right-click and select **Place Grounded at Origin**.

6. Press **Esc** key.

7. Click **Assemble > Component > Place** on the ribbon.

8. Browse to the **Slider Crank Assembly** folder and select all the parts except the **Base**.

9. Click **Open** and click in the graphics window to place the parts.

10. Press **Esc** key.

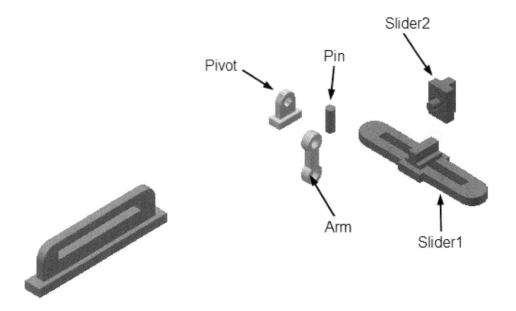

Creating the Slider Joint

1. Click **Assemble > Relationships > Joint** on the ribbon;
    the **Place Joint** dialog box appears.

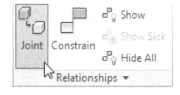

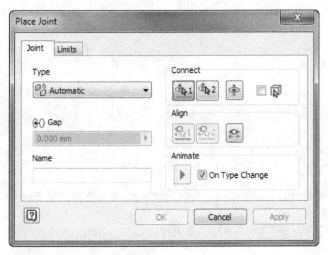

2. Set the **Type** to **Slider**.

3. Select the face on the Slider1 as shown below.

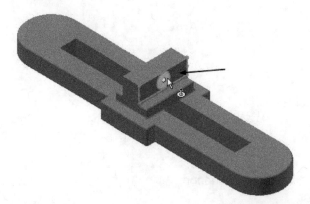

4. Select the face on the Base as shown below; the two faces are aligned.

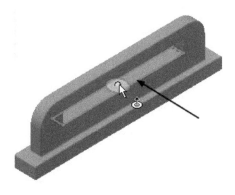

Make sure that the arrow of the joint is along the Y-axis.

5. Click the **Limits** tab on the **Place Joints** dialog box.

6. Select the **Start** and **End** check boxes under the **Linear** group.

7. Set the **Start** to 80 mm and **End** to -80 mm.

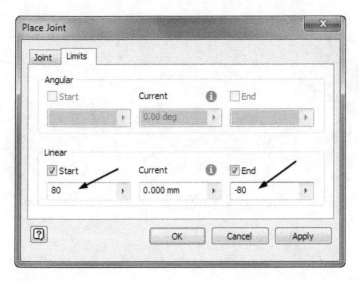

8. Click OK.

9. Select the Slider1 and drag the cursor; the Slider1 slides in the slot of the Base.

10. Click **Assemble > Relationships > Joint** on the ribbon.

11. Set the **Type** to **Slider**.

12. Select the face on the Slider2 as shown below.

13. Select the face on the Slider1 as shown below.

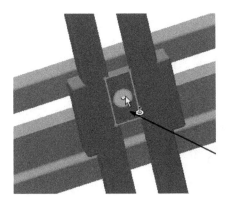

14. Click the **First alignment** button on the dialog box.

15. Select the edge on the Slider2 as shown below.

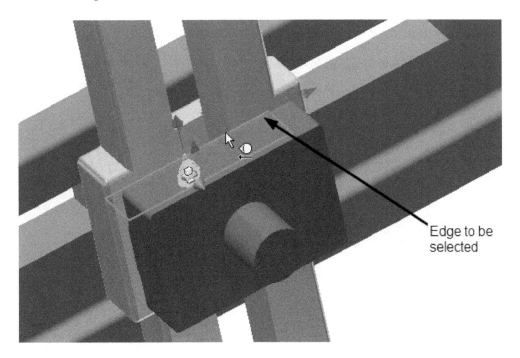

Edge to be selected

16. Select the edge on the Slider1 as shown below.

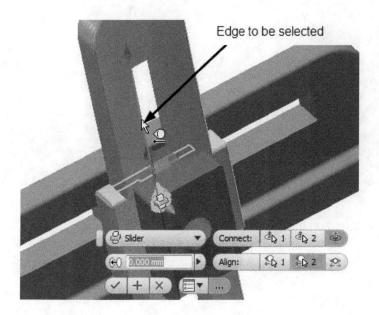

Edge to be selected

17. Click the **Limits** tab.

18. Select the **Start** and **End** check boxes under the **Linear** group.

19. Set the **Start** to 70 mm and **End** to -70 mm.

20. Click OK.

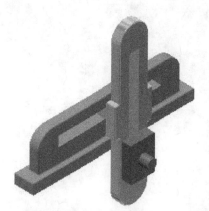

Creating the Rotational Joint

1. Click **Assemble > Relationships > Joint** on the ribbon.

2. Set the **Type** to **Rotational**.

3. Select the circular edge of the arm as shown below.

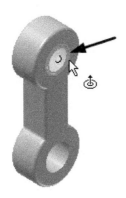

4. Select the circular edge of the Slider2.

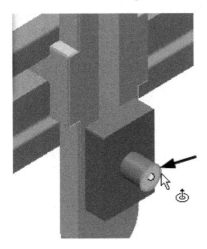

5. Click OK.

Creating the Rigid Joint

1. Click **Assemble > Relationships > Joint** on the ribbon.

Autodesk Inventor Tutorial Book

2. Set the **Type** to **Rigid**.

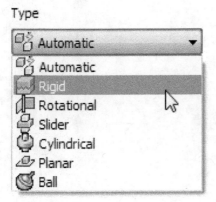

3. Select the top face on the pin.

4. Select the circular edge on the back face of the arm.

5. Click the **Flip Component** button under the **Connect** group.

6. Click OK.

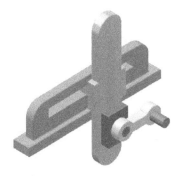

7. Create another rotational joint between the Pin and the Pivot.

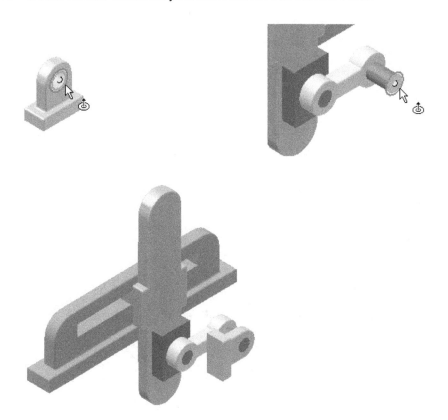

Next, you need to constrain the Pivot by applying constraints.

8. Click the **Assemble** button on the **Relationships** panel.

9. Select **Mate-Flush** from the mini toolbar.

Autodesk Inventor Tutorial Book

10. Select the bottom face of the Pivot and then select the bottom face of the Base.

11. Click **Apply** (plus symbol on the mini toolbar).

12. Select **Mate-Flush** from the mini toolbar.

13. Select the **XZ Plane** of the Pivot and **XZ Plane** of the Base from the **Browser Bar**.

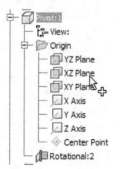

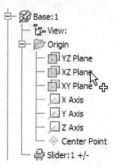

14. Click OK.

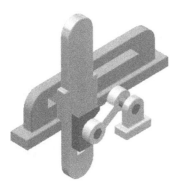

15. Click and drag the arm to view the behavior of the joints.

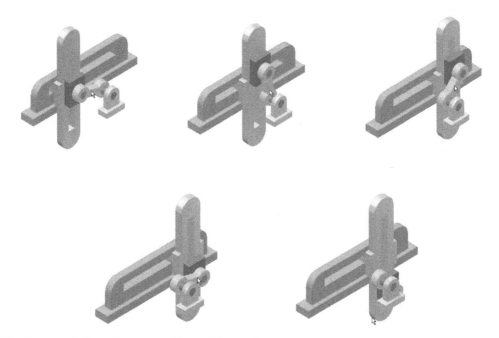

16. Save and close the assembly and its parts.

8. Dimensions and Annotations

In this chapter, you will learn to

- *Create Centerlines and Centermarks*
- *Edit Hatch Pattern*
- *Apply Dimensions*
- *Place Hole callouts*
- *Place Leader Text*
- *Place Datum Feature*
- *Place Feature control frame*
- *Place Surface texture symbol*
- *Modify Title Block Information*

TUTORIAL 1

In this tutorial, you create the drawing shown below.

1. Open a new drawing file using the **ANSI (mm).idw** template.

2. Click **Manage > Styles and Standards > Styles Editor** on the ribbon; the **Style and Standard Editor** dialog box appears.

3. Set the **Projection Type** to **Third Angle**. Click **Done**.

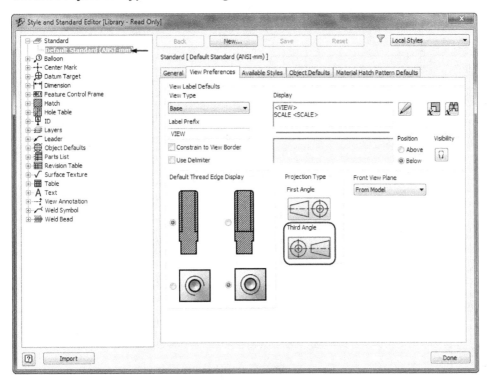

4. Click **Place Views > Create > Base** on the ribbon.

5. Click **Open an existing file** button on the dialog box.

6. Browse to the location of the Adapter Plate created in the Tutorial 1 of the Chapter 5. You can also download this file from the companion website and use it.

7. Set the **Scale** to **5:1**.

8. Set the **Orientation** to **Front**.

9. Set the **Style** to **Hidden Line Removed**.

10. Place the front view on the right-side of the drawing sheet.

11. Right-click and select **OK**.

12. Next, create a section view.
    • Click **Place Views > Create > Section** on the ribbon.
    • Select the front view.
    • Draw the section line on the front view.

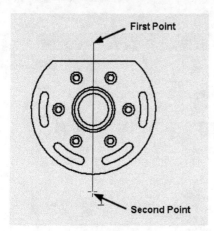

    • Right-click and select **Continue**.
    • Place the section view on the left side.

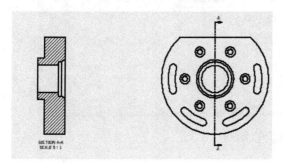

Creating Centerlines and Centermarks

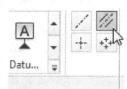

1. Click **Annotate > Symbols > Centerline Bisector** on the ribbon.

2. Select the parallel lines on the section view as shown below; the centerline is created.

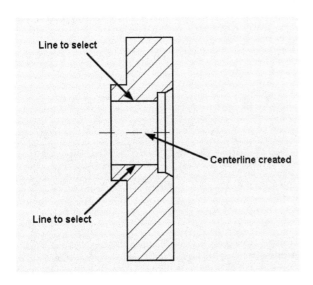

3. Click **Annotate > Symbols > Centerline** on the ribbon.

4. Enter **Shock Base** in the **New Component** Name field.

5. Select the first point and the second point of the centerline as shown below.

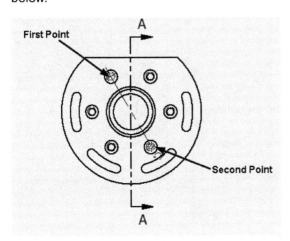

6. Press Esc.

7. Select the centerline to display its end points.

8. Select an end point of the centerline and drag; the centerline is stretched.

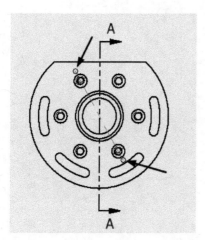

9. Drag the other end point of the center line

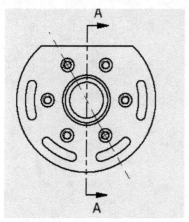

10. Similarly, create other center lines as shown below.

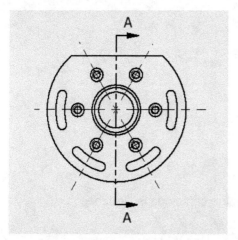

Next, you need to create centermarks.

11. Click **Annotate > Symbols > Centered Pattern** on the ribbon.

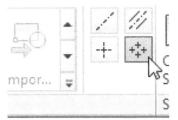

12. Select the center point of the large circle located at the center.

13. Select the end point of the slot located at the right side.

14. Select the end point of the slot located at the left side.

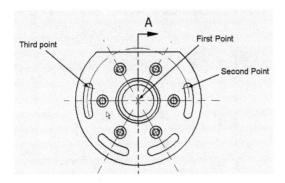

15. Select the end points of all the slots.

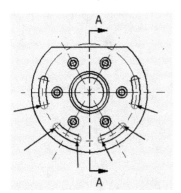

16. Right-click and select **Create** and press **Esc** key.

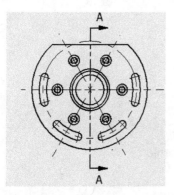

Editing the Hatch Pattern

1. Double-click on the hatch pattern of the section view; the **Edit Hatch Pattern** dialog box appears.

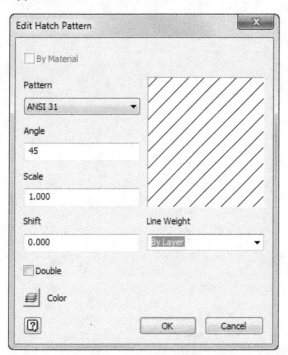

You can select the required hatch pattern from the **Pattern** drop-down. If you select the **Other** option from this drop-down; the **Select Hatch Pattern** dialog box appears. You can select a hatch pattern from this dialog box or load user defined patterns by using the **Load** option. Click **OK** after selecting the required hatch pattern.

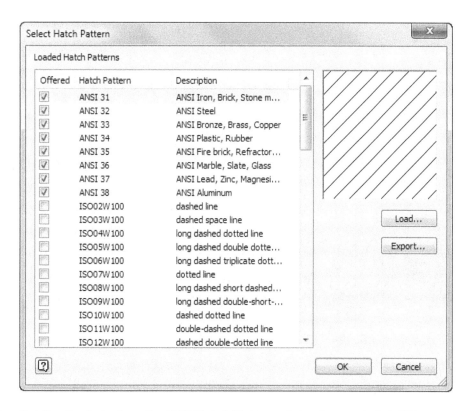

2.   Set the **Scale** to **2** on the **Edit Hatch Pattern** dialog box and click **OK**.

Applying Dimensions

1.   Click **Annotate > Dimension > Dimension** on the ribbon.

2.   Select the center lines on the slot located at the left as shown below.

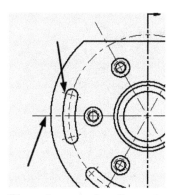

3.   Place the angular dimension; the **Edit Dimension** dialog box appears.

4.   Click the **Precision and Tolerance** tab on the dialog box.

5. Set the **Angular Unit** to **0**.

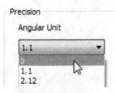

6. Click **OK**.

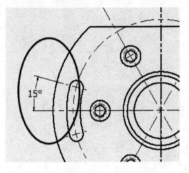

7. Similarly, apply another angular dimension as shown below.

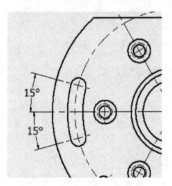

8. Apply angular dimensions between the holes and then between slots.

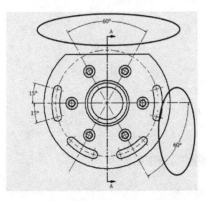

9. Apply the pitch circle diameter of the slots.

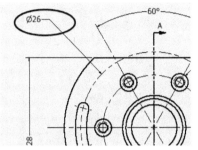

10. With the **Dimension** tool active, select the horizontal line of the front view and the lower quadrant point of the view.

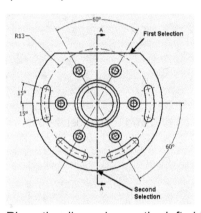

11. Place the dimension on the left side.

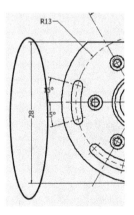

12. Click **Annotate > Feature Notes > Hole and Thread** on the ribbon.

13. Select the counterbore hole and place the hole callout as shown below.

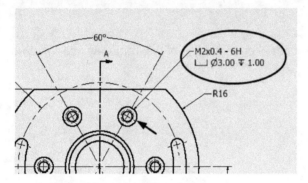

14. Next, create a centered pattern of the counterbore holes and add a dimension to it.

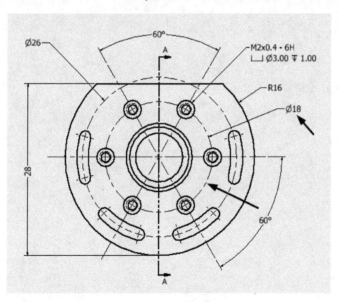

15. Click **Leader Text** on the **Text** panel.

Autodesk Inventor Tutorial Book

16. Select the slot end, as shown below.

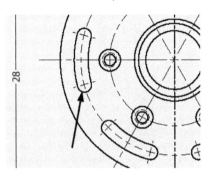

17. Move the cursor away and click.

18. Right-click and select **Continue**; the **Format Text** dialog box appears.

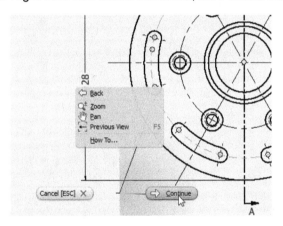

19. Enter the text shown below.

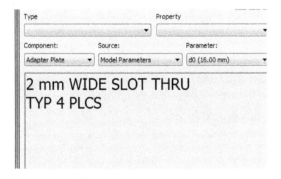

20. Click **OK**. Press **Esc** key.

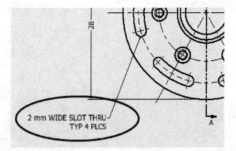

21. Drag and place the section label on the top.

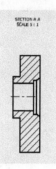

22. Click **Dimension** on the **Dimension** panel.

23. Select the lines as shown below.

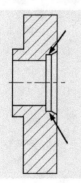

24. Place the dimension; the **Edit Dimension** dialog box appears.

25. Click the **Precision and Tolerance** tab.

26. Set the **Tolerance Method** to **Limits/Fits - Show tolerance**.

27. Set the **Primary Unit** to **0**.

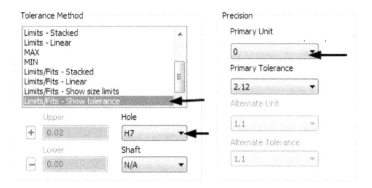

28. Click **OK**.

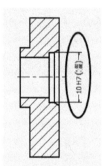

29. Similarly, apply the other dimensions as shown below. You can also use the **Retrieve Dimensions** tool to apply the dimensions.

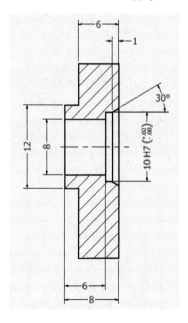

Placing the Datum Feature

1. Click **Annotate > Symbols > Datum Feature** on the ribbon.

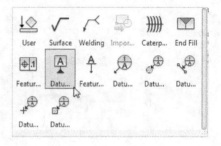

2. Select the extension line of the dimension as shown below.

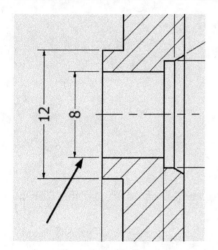

3. Move the cursor downward and click.

4. Move the cursor toward left and click; the **Format Text** dialog box appears. Make sure that **A** is entered in the dialog box.

5. Click OK.

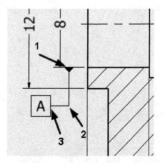

---

6. Similarly, place a datum feature B as shown below. Press Esc.

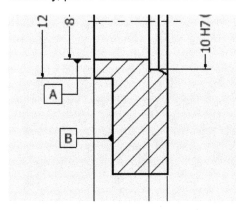

Placing the Feature Control Frame

1. Click **Annotate > Symbols > Feature Control Frame** on the ribbon.

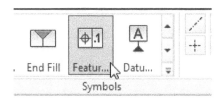

2. Select a point on the line as shown below.

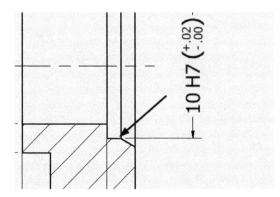

3. Move the cursor horizontally toward right and click.

4. Right-click and select **Continue**; the **Feature Control Frame** dialog box appears.

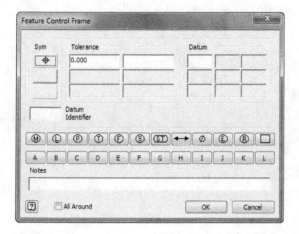

5.   Click the **Sym** button and select **Circular Run-out**.

6.   Enter **0.02** in the **Tolerance** box and **A** in the **Datum** box.

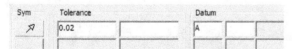

7.   Click **OK**. Right-click and select **Cancel**.

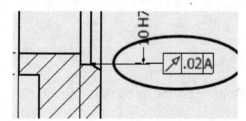

Placing the Surface Texture Symbols

1.   Click **Annotate > Symbols > Surface Texture Symbol** on the ribbon.

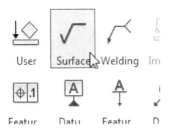

2. Click on the inner cylindrical face of the hole as shown below.

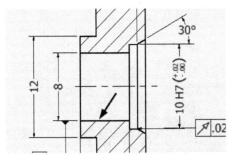

3. Right-click and select **Continue**; the **Surface Texture** dialog box appears.

4. Set the **Roughness Average - maximum value** to **63**.

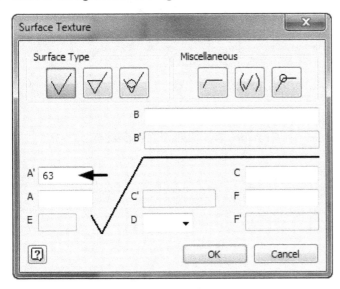

5. Click **OK**. Right-click and select **Cancel**.

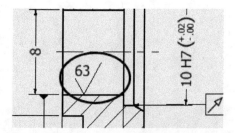

6.   Apply the other annotations of the drawing. The final drawing is shown below.

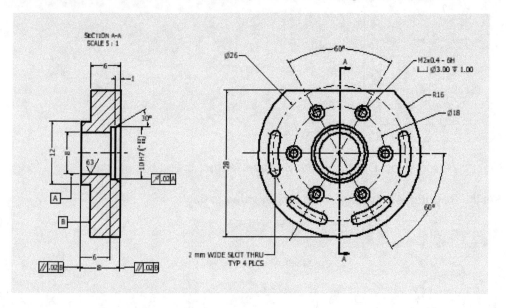

Modifying the Title Block Information

1.   Right-click on the **Adapter Plate** in the **Browser Bar**. Select **iProperties**.

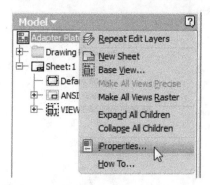

2.   Click the **Summary** tab and enter the information as shown next.

You can also update the Project information, drawing status and other custom information in the respective tabs.

3. Click **OK**.

4. Save the file.

5. To export the file to AutoCAD format, click **Application Menu > Export > Export to DWG**. Click **Save**.

6. Close the file.